7 SECRETS
OF A
HEALTHY
DATING
RELATIONSHIP

Books by Les Parrott III

*Helping the Struggling Adolescent: A Guide to
   Thirty Common Problems for Parents, Counselors,
   and Youth Workers*

Helping the Struggling Adolescent: A Counseling Guide

*Love's Unseen Enemy: Overcoming Guilt
   to Build Healthy Relationships*

*The Career Counselor: Charting Your
   Lifelong Career Path* (with Leslie Parrott)

*Saving Your Marriage Before It Starts:
   Seven Questions to Ask Before
   (and After) You Marry* (with Leslie Parrott)

The Marriage Mentor Manual (with Leslie Parrott)

*Becoming Soul Mates: Cultivating Spiritual Intimacy
   in the Early Years of Marriage* (with Leslie Parrott)

7 SECRETS OF A HEALTHY DATING RELATIONSHIP

LES PARROTT III

A leader's guide is available
from your local bookstore or from your publisher.

Beacon Hill Press of Kansas City
Kansas City, Missouri

Copyright 1995 by Beacon Hill Press of Kansas City

ISBN 083-411-5549

Printed in the United States of America

Edited by Becki Privett

Cover design by Paul Franitza

Library of Congress Cataloging-in-Publication Data

Parrott, Les.
    7 secrets of a healthy dating relationship / Les Parrott III.
       p. cm.
    ISBN 0-8341-1554-9
    1. Dating (Social customs) 2. Dating (Social customs)—Religious aspects—Christianity. 3. Man-woman relationships. I. Title.
HQ801.P338   1995   95-2-422
306.73—dc20   CIP

10 9 8 7 6 5

To Andrew, Justin, Grady, and Madison

Contents

Contents

Foreword

Ever feel more at ease interacting with your computer screen or Walkman than with other people? Relationships. We know they are important. We know they take time and energy. Often, though, we're not very good at building them. Many of us have failed, and many of us are still hurting. Too many relationships fall apart. Add to this the fact that we live in a mobile society. Friends are constantly moving, or maybe we're the ones who move. It's no wonder many of us hesitate to make new friends. It's just too much trouble really getting close to someone, if there's a strong chance we'll lose them. Yes, it's much easier interacting with our high-tech toys than risking relationships today.

Building healthy relationships is what this book is about. Healthy relationships not only energize our lives and help us grow as caring, compassionate individuals, but living in relationship with others is how God designed us to be. As you read this book, take hold of the helpful insights for strengthening your ability to relate to others. You won't find a load of ideas for date planning in this book. What you *will* find are ways to develop your character, your inner person, by using biblical truths to evaluate all your close relationships.

Les Parrott III is uniquely qualified to help you learn to build healthy relationships. He understands the struggles of today. His extensive research in the area of relationship continues to result in helpful books and articles. He teaches in the school of social and behavioral sciences and the Department of Psychology at Seattle Pacific University. Les is also a frequent speaker at conventions and other gatherings. He is the kind of person you would enjoy getting to know—one who listens, laughs, and loves life. Undoubtedly, relationships are important to this man. I count it a privilege to call him my friend.

As you read this book, have your marker ready to highlight statements that raise questions for you. Talk over those questions with a friend, pastor, or parent. Use the book in small-group sessions at your church or school. And commit yourself to follow the insights you gain to build God-honoring relationships.

—Fred Fullerton
Director of
Nazarene Youth International Ministries

Preface

Choosing whom to date—and ultimately finding true love—is one of the most important decisions you will ever make. It can be done by impulse, driven by misinformation from others. Or it can be done through a thoughtful process, guided by proven principles. This book will help you do just that. It identifies some of the most important biblical principles for building loving relationships with members of the opposite sex.

7 Secrets to Healthy Dating Relationships is for anyone interested in building close relationships. Whether you're looking for someone to date, already in a relationship, or even considering marriage, *7 Secrets* reveals seven powerful ways for both becoming and finding people with whom you can build healthy relationships.

Spaced throughout the book are several self-tests to help you assess particular qualities in yourself and in the people you date. They are designed to help you apply the message of each chapter.

Another feature of each chapter is "Something to Think and Talk About." This section provides several questions about the chapter for personal reflection or for group discussion.

Each chapter ends with a suggestion for further personal study of the topic. Should you be interested, there is also an accompanying leader's guide for small groups to discuss the message of *7 Secrets*.

I would contradict my chapter on gratitude if I failed to express appreciation to Fred Fullerton, Mark Brown, Mark Gilroy, Becki Privett, Steve Moore, and my wife, Leslie. They all had a part in this project.

John Woodyard, Drew Anderson, and the board who

worked with us at the Murdock Charitable Trust deserve special appreciation for helping Leslie and me establish the Center for Relationship Development on the campus of Seattle Pacific University. This book will serve as another tool in the center's mission to foster healthy relationships.

Please let me know how things go in your pilgrimage. Send correspondence to: Dr. Les Parrott III, Center for Relationship Development, Seattle Pacific University, Seattle, WA 98119.

◆ 1 ◆

Guess What—It's No Secret!

DO YOU REMEMBER the first time you ever said, "I love you," in a romantic way? I do. I was in the third grade. I had a wild crush on a fourth grader named Laurie. We were in the same Sunday School class on an outing to play miniature golf when my true feelings for her unexpectedly surfaced.

While my buddies were concentrating on knocking a golf ball through a turning windmill, I couldn't help but be distracted by Laurie. I don't think I actually talked to her, or she to me, but I sometimes smiled at Laurie across the miniature greens, and she giggled with embarrassment.

After 18 holes of the most romantic golf game I've ever played, I managed to sit next to Laurie in our Sunday School teacher's car for the ride home. Laurie was on my right, and Bruce, a good friend, was on my left. On our drive back to the church where our parents would pick us up, however, we had a minor fender bender. No one was seriously injured, but I chipped my tooth on the back of the front seat.

As we were looking for the piece of my tooth that had broken off, Bruce discovered it stuck in the side of his neck! The tooth trauma, however, was only the beginning. A police officer who had arrived on the scene examined my lower lip through the car window and said, "Looks like you're going to need a couple of stitches there, pal." I touched my lip and discovered it was bleeding.

Blood! *My* blood! I couldn't believe it. My heart raced, and my short life flashed before me. I knew it was only a matter of moments before I would die. With what I thought would be my last breath, I looked at Laurie, tossed my self-concern aside, threw my arms around her, and in front of all my buddies said, "Laurie, I love you!"

Dating Styles

Well, I obviously didn't die in that minor automobile accident, but I'm still a little wounded from the embarrassment. Feelings of love are powerful. As a counselor, I have worked with hundreds of young people trying to understand the confusing emotions of love through the dating process. I have observed that some people have a distinct attitude as they approach the realm of dating. Some of these approaches will sound familiar:

The Whiners. You'll usually find this group of daters complaining. They can think of dozens of reasons not to go out on a date: "I don't have enough money." "I wouldn't know what to talk about." "Nobody ever asks me, and I can't ask a guy." "I don't have a car." The list of excuses goes on and on for whiners.

The Definers. This group of daters want to know exactly where they stand in a relationship. They have their own dating language. They assign degrees of seriousness to a date by repeating their words. For example, they will ask, "Is this a date or a *date*-date?" "Does he like you, or does he *like you*-like you?" "Was it a kiss or a *kiss*-kiss?" Definers want to know where they stand.

The Clock-watchers. I feel sorry for this group of daters. You can almost see the minutes ticking away on their faces. They are on the verge of panic, believing time is running out on finding a person to date. They don't usually express their fear directly, though. A group of young men I was having lunch with were complaining about never having a date, when a young woman walked by. One of the guys followed her with his eyes, paused, and said, "She wants me." Sometimes those who appear most confident are the ones who are most afraid of being left dateless.

The Spiritualizers. This group of daters is usually very patient. They are diligently looking for "that special someone." They are searching for a dramatic sign—a spiritual revelation—to convince them that *this* is the person they are to date. They are earnest about the dating process but are often so cautious that they overlook good opportunities.

These are only a few of the most common dating styles. Young people cope with the dating dilemma in dozens of other ways as well. I'm not knocking any of them. Unfortunately, however, too many young people discover, after an initial ride on love's cloud nine, that things just didn't work out.

You'll be pleased to know there's no secret formula for success. Everyone can build loving relationships.

Relationships that start and end badly can leave a person disappointed, depressed, bitter, and even wounded. Yes, we need all the help we can get when it comes to dating.

So what *can* we do to ease the agony of dating? That's what 7 *Secrets of a Healthy Dating Relationship* is all about. You'll be pleased to know there's no secret formula for success. Everyone can build loving relationships. In fact, you may already be effectively using some of the principles given here to help you.

Swimming Upstream

Dating isn't easy. But then, neither is swimming upstream. I talked with a young person recently who was struggling with the whole "dating thing," who in frustration said to me, "Wouldn't it be easier if, instead of dating, we could just swim upstream like salmon—or make loud clacking noises in the woods?"

I understand his frustration. Each year huge numbers of salmon find their way from the Pacific Ocean up the rivers of Washington, Oregon, and Idaho to the spawning grounds where their offspring are born. Many fish get sidetracked and perish in canals or ditches before the peace and solitude of the headwaters is reached.

Similarly, many dating relationships become doomed because someone lost his or her direction. Before we resort to any further comparisons from the animal kingdom, let's explore some other readily available alternatives. I hope 7 *Secrets* will help you avoid the most treacherous waters. It's designed to help you chart a course by marking the way with seven biblical qualities that lead to true love.

Before we begin uncovering these secrets, let's address the number one anxiety-producing question surrounding the dating process: *How can I be sure the person I am dating is right for me?* That's a good question. How would *you* answer it? I tend to think that knowing what characteristics you appreciate in other people may make a big difference in finding the "right" people to date. Take a moment to write down at least eight characteristics you look for in a potential date:

1. _____

2. _____

3. _____

4. _____

5. _____

6. _____

7. _____

8. _____

As you look at the list you just made, circle the three qualities that are most important to you. Now, do you think that if a person you are dating has these three qualities, it means he or she is "right" for you? Still a bit uncertain?

You aren't alone. Let's unlock a few secrets.

So What's the Big Secret?

I've read most of the hundreds of helpful articles and dozens of useful books on dating. Rather than telling you what other writers and researchers are saying about dating, I've decided to let 7 Secrets focus on what Scripture has to say. You may say, "Wait a minute. Where in Scripture is dating discussed?" You're right. Dating wasn't a part of either the Old Testament or New Testament cultures, but building relationships was. This book is built on seven relationship-friendly qualities found in seven verses from Ephesians (5:15-21):

> Be very careful, then, how you live—not as unwise but as wise, making the most of every opportunity, because the days are evil. Therefore do not be foolish, but understand what the Lord's will is. Do not get drunk on wine, which leads to debauchery. Instead, be filled with the Spirit. Speak to one another with psalms, hymns and spiritual songs. Sing and make music in your heart to the Lord, always giving thanks to God the Father for everything, in the name of our Lord Jesus Christ. Submit to one another out of reverence for Christ.

This passage, when studied carefully, reveals important personal qualities that apply in building healthy dating relationships. These qualities are

Wisdom

Optimism

Discernment

Spirituality

Joyfulness

Gratitude

Empathy

Each of these characteristics will be discussed in the

chapters that follow. If your personal list of desirable characteristics for a dating partner does not match the ones outlined in this book, don't let it get to you. It doesn't mean your list is wrong. However, the list derived from this passage of Scripture contains the "secrets" for finding true love, not just in dating, but in all your relationships. And it can work for you.

Getting Started

This book is designed to help you confidently identify signs of growth and maturity in the people you're interested in dating. Part of that design includes challenging you, getting you to evaluate your dating life, introducing you to scripture that focuses on relationships, and encouraging you to discuss dating with others. Here's how it will happen:

Beginning with the next chapter, you will receive from me a challenge to make personal the "secret" you've just read about by incorporating it into your standards for dating.

Self-tests. As you discover each new secret, you'll encounter a questionnaire you can use to evaluate your relationship carefully to know if Cupid's dart has hit a bull's-eye or missed the target entirely. Take each self-test twice. The first time, rate yourself to see the extent to which you've applied that secret to your life. Then rate the person you're interested in dating. As you do this, remember that all people, yourself included, have the potential for change. So the rating you give someone may not be the final word for that person. Use the tests as a guide to see where you might need to grow. Along the way, these self-tests may also introduce you to qualities you never knew could exist in a person.

Something to Think and Talk About. This helpful addition to each chapter will help you dialogue about dating with others. You'll be able to move away from your own experience and begin to gather information about what others are doing in their dating relationships. It's an important part of learning how to build healthy relationships.

For Further Study. At the end of each chapter you'll find additional scripture that supports the secret of that chapter. Prepare in advance to have a Bible handy when you come to the end of a chapter. Consider using a Bible concordance for other verses on the importance of relationships. Look up words like *friend, friendship,* and *companion.*

OK, now we're ready to begin—or as the salmon might say, *dive in!*

· 2 ·

Being a Wise Guy

*Be very careful, then, how you live—not as
unwise but as wise.*—EPH. 5:15

JENNY, A JUNIOR in high school, had a wild crush on Steve, a
senior. When Steve admitted he was head over heels about her,
too, life couldn't get any better. They started dating immediately and discovered they had a lot in common. Their times together were always fun. They attended the same church and
had many of the same friends. Everyone thought Jenny and
Steve made a great couple.

They had been dating for about four months when something unexpected happened in their relationship. It was two
months before graduation. All year Steve had been planning to
attend a university in Kansas that had offered him an excellent
basketball scholarship. He had a good grade-point average and
good SAT scores, but his ability to shoot hoops was the reason
this university was wanting to pay for his undergraduate degree.

Like the rest of the seniors, Steve seemed excited about
college, but not quite *as* excited. He was concerned with how
the upcoming changes in his life would affect this new relationship with Jenny. It was on their seventh or eighth date
when Steve began talking with Jenny about the future—*their*
future. He said something that left Jenny speechless.

"I really care about you, Jen," he told her while sitting in a restaurant booth. "And I've got to know if you will marry me. Will you?"

Jenny was stunned. She didn't know what to say. She liked Steve a lot. She had even plastered his name all over most of her notebooks. But marriage! Why think of marriage *now*, after only eight dates?

Jenny avoided giving Steve a direct answer to his pressing question. Granted, even though she knew the proposal was premature, she was flattered. It was a tough ride home after their date at the restaurant. As Steve drove her home, he told her that if she would marry him, he would give up his scholarship and get a job to save money so they could marry soon after her graduation. "We wouldn't even have to tell anyone about our plan," Steve whispered.

Jenny was confused. In the driveway of her house she again deflected Steve's question and said good-night. She didn't tell her parents about Steve's proposal. She didn't tell her girl-friends at church or school. She simply knew it was a silly request and out of the question for her. She felt deeply for Steve, but she also knew it was terribly unwise to give in to strong emotions without sound judgment.

In looking at these two young people's actions, it appears that Steve, even if wise in other areas of his life, didn't exercise wisdom in this instance. Jenny, on the other hand, did.

A Crazy Little Thing Called Love

Falling in love is a dizzying experience. Solomon's Song of Songs says, "Many waters cannot quench love; rivers cannot wash it away" (8:7). Once the spark of attraction catches flame, love can quickly turn into a raging fire. Engulfed by its heat, people sometimes are oblivious to sound judgment.

Love really can cause some people to lose their heads. They become "crazy in love." They become compelled by the emotional force of love and give up their ability to analyze the situation. I read recently about a man who hired a helicopter to drop 2,500 carnations and 10,000 love letters onto the lawn of a woman he loved. Apparently the woman failed to share this man's affection and had him charged with littering. She told reporters he had "lost his mind."

When it comes to building lasting relationships, wisdom—the ability to reason with insight—is essential.

It is a common danger. The compelling emotional force can override our capacity to think clearly if we let it. That's the key—*if we let it.* I believe this is why Scripture says, "Be very careful, then, how you live—not as unwise but as wise" (Eph. 5:15). So here's our first secret: **When it comes to building lasting relationships, wisdom—the ability to reason with insight—is essential.**

Two Common Myths About Wisdom

Wisdom belongs to the old and experienced. What do you think of when you hear the word *wisdom?* Perhaps you think of an older person, a sage with gray hair, a long beard, and small, round glasses. Toss those common caricatures of wisdom out the window. They don't present an accurate picture.

Wisdom doesn't always have to come with age. It is not something you have wait to receive when you are old enough. If that were so, Prov. 4:5-10 wouldn't tell us to get wisdom at all costs. We can make wise choices now. God expects us to. Wisdom is something we can constantly exercise and develop.

Only smart people can be considered wise. Contrary to popular belief, wisdom is not automatic with one who has a high IQ. Rev. Paul Smyth graduated with honors from the esteemed Cambridge University. He was considered a mental giant. But consider for yourself how wise he was.

Upon graduation from Cambridge, Rev. Smyth became a British pastor. Spending the majority of his time studying in the library instead of ministering to the needs of his people, his congregation steadily dwindled in attendance until one Sunday no member of his congregation turned up for morning worship—not even one. Was he wise? I'm sure many of you will agree that while Rev. Smyth may have been a brilliant man, he was definitely an unwise pastor.

So then, since you don't have to be in your twilight years and you don't even have to get straight A's to be wise, what do you have to do? A dictionary definition may help us here. The *American Heritage Dictionary* tells us wisdom is "a common sense understanding of what is true, right, or lasting." Did you catch that? It is built on common sense. Unfortunately for many, it appears that Horace Greeley was right when he said, "Common sense is very uncommon."

Why Do I Need Wisdom?

A maid, preparing to serve mushrooms to a group of high-class, distinguished ladies, asked the hostess if there was any possibility that the mushrooms were poisonous. Unsure, the hostess suggested that she feed some of the mushrooms to the dog as a test. She did, and nothing happened. However, in the middle of the meal the maid came in and frantically told the hostess the dog was dead. In a panic, the hostess called in an emergency team of paramedics to work on her guests. Halfway through the process the hostess asked the maid, "Did the dog suffer?" "No," answered the maid. "He was run over by a car."

One good reason we all need wisdom is because wisdom is the common sense that helps us avoid embarrassing mistakes. Those who exercise wisdom don't jump to conclusions or make rash decisions without gathering the facts.

Steve, from the story at the beginning of this chapter, felt the exhilaration of infatuation and expected it to last forever. He wanted to plan his whole future around the small piece of information that mattered most to him at the moment: being with Jenny made him feel great.

Wisdom is needed for guidance in a relationship if it is expected to be based on more than exciting feelings. Romantic feelings eventually fade. And exercising wisdom doesn't mean the relationship is doomed to failure. Wisdom has been known actually to fan the flame of initial infatuation, helping a relationship grow strong and healthy. Where romance focuses on emotions, wisdom deals with character.

Wisdom is the common sense that helps us avoid embarrassing mistakes.

Wisdom is taken seriously in Scripture. Its warnings are clear. If you shrug off wisdom, you can't be certain of protection from disaster. Consider these words from chapter 4 of Proverbs:

> When I was a boy in my father's house, still tender, and an only child of my mother, he taught me and said, "Lay hold of my words with all your heart; keep my commands and you will live. Get wisdom, get understanding; do not forget my words or swerve from them. Do not forsake wisdom, and she will protect you; love her, and she will watch over you. Wisdom is supreme; therefore get wisdom. Though it cost all you have, get understanding. Esteem her, and she will exalt you; embrace her, and she will honor you. She will set a garland of grace on your head and present you with a crown of splendor" (vv. 3-9).

This passage is an expression of the importance of the commonsense wisdom we all learn from parents, teachers, and others as we mature. Those who ignore wisdom will almost assuredly bring disaster on themselves (Prov. 1:20-27). No healthy person craves disaster. You can see why it's important for you and the person you're interested in dating to take wisdom seriously.

Finding a Wise Date

Wisdom can sometimes be difficult to spot in others. Job,

in the Old Testament, asked, "Where can wisdom be found? Where does understanding dwell?" (28:12). He discovered, as we do in our search for it, that wisdom isn't about ways of *doing,* but rather about ways of *being.* Wisdom is not an action. Its work is done long before we ever say wise words or do wise deeds. Wisdom is what helps us behave a certain way. It generally emerges over time in hundreds of ways great and small.

Where romance focuses on emotions, wisdom deals with character.

In yet another call to get wisdom, the writer of Proverbs compared searching for wisdom to mining and said, "If you look for it as for silver and search for it as for hidden treasure, then you will understand" (2:4-5). To guide you on your own treasure expedition, let's explore some of the most important characteristics of a wise person.

1. The Wise Date Has More Humility than Pride

My wife, Leslie, and I (yes, we have the same name) once double-dated in downtown Chicago with our friends Kevin and Kathy. We had a great time at one of Chicago's famous pizza shops. On the way home, since Lakeshore Drive was jammed with traffic, Kevin and I decided to take a "short-cut." Kevin drove. I navigated. In mere minutes we were lost.

You guessed it. The often tragic aspect of the male psyche, the aspect that refuses to ask for directions, emerged. We were too proud to admit we couldn't find our way. In short, our pride landed us in one of the most dangerous sections of Chicago, the infamous Cabrini Green. Cabrini Green is known for its high-rise apartments for the poor—which isn't so bad; but it's also known for gang violence and drive-by shootings— which is *real* bad. Thankfully, a patrol car spotted us, and a big Irish Chicago cop escorted us back to Michigan Avenue and to landmarks we knew. We breathed a collective sigh of relief, while Kevin and I felt foolish for not asking for help.

"A prudent question," asserted Francis Bacon, "is one-half of wisdom." Knowing what you know is great, but knowing (and admitting) what you don't know—that's wisdom. That double date showed me how wisdom includes being humble enough to admit what you don't know. Socrates said, "The wisest man is he who knows his own ignorance." When we let pride take over, Prov. 11:2 tells us, disgrace is not far behind.

> **A prudent question is one-half of wisdom.**
>
> —Francis Bacon

Humility, on the other hand, never leaves you open for embarrassment. So when you're looking for someone with whom to build a close relationship, ask yourself if developing humility is something you need to work on in your own life, and then notice if the person you're interested in has a problem asking for help.

2. The Wise Date Is Authentic, Not Deceptive

Being a sculptor in ancient Rome was a respected profession. People had not yet "arrived" unless their home was adorned with statues. Not all sculptors, however, had the same skills or sense of beauty. A second-rate sculptor would cover his mistakes with wax. They became so good at "remolding" with wax that most people could not tell the difference with the naked eye. If you wanted to be sure your statue was authentic, you would go to the artisan in the marketplace who displayed the sign marked *sine cera*—without wax.

More than any other virtue we look for in people, we value *sincerity*—without wax. We respect individuals who represent the real thing. Those kinds of people are not always easy to find. Many, especially in the initial stages of getting to know someone, can come across as something they aren't. They masquerade their flaws and defects. People spend hours preparing for a date, arranging their hair, choosing clothes, spraying perfume—filling their faults with wax. Why? Does this behavior let our date know what we *really* are? Of course not. We approach dates as times when we all try to look our best.

A date is often a showcase, designed to show only our best side and conceal our shortcomings. Young men and women can be obsessed with how to look, what to say, how to eat. For this reason it is particularly important to look beyond the veneer of exteriors for someone who is genuine. For example, ask yourself: Does this person have sincere intentions about this relationship, or is it merely a show? Is this person interested in me as a person or as an object? Am I being used? Can I be myself with this person, or am I caught up in his or her deception?

This may not be something you can discover on the first or even second date. Granted, while getting to know each other takes time, it's important to make every effort in the earliest stages of a relationship to show your true self to someone with whom you want to build a close relationship.

3. The Wise Date Knows the Difference Between True Love and Infatuation

I often encounter young people like Steve who, after being caught up in the excitement of a new relationship, make the mistake of confusing infatuation with love. Who can blame them? Infatuation is a wonderful, exhilarating experience. It seems as though the good feelings will last forever. They don't last—and, more importantly, aren't ever *meant* to last.

Infatuation has a place. It's what draws us to each other. But anyone who has developed a lasting, true love for and with someone knows that you cannot live on the top of an emotional mountain day after day.

The feelings stirred up in infatuation swing from high to low to high in cyclical rhythm. And since romantic excitement is an emotion, it too will oscillate. *Real love takes time to build.* Jenny had enough patient wisdom to understand that when Steve was impatient.

But how, then, can real love be distinguished from temporary infatuation? There are several characteristics that separate true love from infatuation. Infatuation is based on one or maybe two physical characteristics or shared interests; love is based on the whole person. Infatuation is instant; love grows slowly like fruit on a tree. Infatuation's bubble can be burst in an instant. Love, on the other hand, is a commitment based on the realities of the imperfections of both people involved. Ultimately, infatuation meets *my* needs—while love meets *our* needs.

I agree with the answer James Dobson gives to the question of how love can be discerned from infatuation: "There is only one answer to those questions: It takes time." (Longer than Jenny and Steve's eight dates!) Dobson also advises that any couple contemplating marriage (or any other important decision) should make no important, life-shaping decisions quickly or impulsively, and when in doubt, should stall for time.

So take your time. Look carefully for someone with whom to build a close relationship. And while you're looking, look for someone who also embodies this same kind of wise patience.

4. *The Wise Date Has a Spiritual Dimension*

Not far from my home is a church that places a sign on their lawn every Christmas season that reads, "Wise men still seek Him." I like that.

Wise persons always seek God's wisdom. Human wisdom on its own is inadequate. In fact, human wisdom never could comprehend God's plan for salvation (see 1 Cor. 1:19, 21; 3:18-19). "Knowledge is horizontal," declared evangelist Billy Graham. Then he added: "Wisdom is vertical—it comes down from above." Spiritual wisdom is given by the Holy Spirit. In the Old Testament era, Solomon exemplified spiritual wisdom (Matt. 12:42). When Jesus came, His wisdom outshone the wisdom of others (13:54). When leaders became necessary in the Jerusalem church, people selected those who possessed spiritual wisdom (Acts 6:3).

Look for someone who is seeking spiritual wisdom. Avoid getting involved in relationships with those who feel they have already achieved spiritual greatness. They haven't. And while you're looking, spend time in God's Word.

So then, a wise person is humble, sincere, patient, and a perpetual student of God's wisdom. Every Christian can ask God for wisdom, and He will give it to him or her (James 1:5). Wisdom is found in the Savior. It is no wonder the psalmist said: "The fear of the LORD is the beginning of wisdom" (111:10; see also Prov. 9:10).

So this is my first challenge to you: When building relationships, be and look for someone who exercises wisdom.

SELF-TEST

Take this self-test twice—once for yourself to evaluate whether you're developing wisdom, and once to get some idea of how much your date (actual or potential) possesses the components of wisdom discussed in this chapter.

Take your time as you think about these questions, and remember that these results are not the final word on your relationships. People can change. This test is only to help you better evaluate your relationship.

Choose only one answer for each question.

Do you consider yourself humble?
1. _____ Not at all. I'm cocky.
2. _____ Yes! Too humble!
3. _____ Somewhat humble.
4. _____ Very humble in a healthy way.

What about sincerity?
1. _____ Not at all. I'm a phony.
2. _____ It's hard to know for sure.
3. _____ Somewhat sincere.
4. _____ Very authentic and sincere.

Do you consider yourself a patient person?
1. _____ No, I make things happen even when I'm not ready.
2. _____ Sometimes. I can wait for some things, but not others.
3. _____ I try to be patient when I can and let things happen.
4. _____ I'm a very patient person. I never initiate anything without thinking it through first.

Do you consider yourself to be spiritually grounded?
1. _____ Not at all. I'm not a Christian.
2. _____ I try to be spiritual but often am not.
3. _____ I'm somewhat spiritually grounded.
4. _____ I'm a committed Christian who seeks wisdom from God.

Scoring

Tally the four items. There is a possible range of scores from 4 to 16. The higher the score, the more you see yourself or your date possessing the components of wisdom. Keep this questionnaire in proper perspective. Wisdom could never be reduced to a number. Think of it as a way to help you clarify your thinking.

Something to Think and Talk About

- Do you think Jenny made the right decision by not rushing into a committed relationship with Steve? Why or why not?
- In your own words, how would you describe wisdom?

- What do you look for in a person to help you know that he or she is sincere?
- An ancient Chinese proverb says, "Patience is power. With time and patience the mulberry leaf becomes silk." How can patience increase the beauty and value of a dating relationship?
- This chapter noted humility, sincerity, patience, and spirituality as important components of wisdom. What other qualities do you think might be a part of being wise?

For Further Study

Use a topical study Bible or a concordance to explore the biblical teaching of wisdom. There are many verses that further expound on wisdom. Concentrate on these books: Psalms, Proverbs, and James.

· 3 ·

The Hot-water Test

Mak[e] the most of every opportunity, because the days are evil.—EPH. 5:16

BEFORE WE WERE MARRIED, Leslie took me on a date to celebrate my 19th birthday. On an August evening we drove for nearly an hour to one of my favorite restaurants. When we arrived, the hostess told us it would be more than an hour's wait. "That's OK," Leslie cheerfully piped up. "We can put our name on the list and celebrate your birthday in the parking lot while we wait."

As we headed back to the car, Leslie instructed me, "Unlock the trunk and then sit in the front seat with your eyes closed." She was grinning from ear to ear. I took my assigned position and heard a rustling commotion from the open trunk. Leslie, I was about to learn, had baked a chocolate cake and secretly placed it in the trunk along with her birthday present to me.

Before I tell you what happened next, let's make sure you have an accurate picture of the situation. Leslie had taken a delicate chocolate cake with creamy icing on an hour-long ride in the trunk of an automobile in the middle of August in Illinois. This was now one very hot cake!

As Leslie precariously balanced the jiggly cake on a glass platter in one hand, she awkwardly managed to carry her present to me in the other. She came around the end of the car and somehow scooted into the passenger side without dropping her precarious cargo. With my eyes closed (and only peeking a little), I saw Leslie maneuver into the car successfully. But as she placed the cake on her lap, it quickly slid off the platter and onto her yellow dress!

At that moment I raised my right eyelid and knew that we had a problem. I did everything I could to stifle the laugh that was gurgling in my windpipe. This was the funniest thing I had witnessed in a very long time.

I laughed uncontrollably for only a moment or two, but it didn't take long for Leslie to share in the fun by scooping up a fistful of chocolate cake off her dress and smearing it on my white pants. That's when I learned Leslie knew what it means to make the most of every situation—even when you've lost control of the situation!

I'm not sure this is exactly what the writer of Ephesians had in mind when he said, "Make the most of every opportunity" (5:16, TLB), but I do know that people who know how to make the most of an opportunity are terrific to be around. When things don't go as planned, they know how to seize and maximize the moment. These kinds of people are usually termed optimists.

What Is Optimism?

Martin Seligman at the University of Pennsylvania has probably done more to help us understand optimism than anyone. As a 21-year-old graduate fresh out of college, he observed an experiment that sent him on a quest to find out why some people seek opportunity while others give up.

In the experiment Dr. Seligman observes, dogs were subjected to a minor shock, which they could avoid by jumping over a low wall that separated two sides of a shuttle box. Most dogs learned this task easily. But other dogs just lay down whimpering. They had no will to try. When Seligman investigated the dogs who had given up, he found they had been used in a prior experiment in which they received shocks no matter what they did. These dogs had "learned" helplessness. Because they had been given shocks regardless of whether they struggled or jumped or barked or did nothing, they learned that nothing they did mattered. So why try?

Mark Twain said, "There is no sadder sight than an old pessimist, except a young pessimist." Like the dogs in this experiment, some people learn to give up. They actually work at thinking pessimistically. The three defining characteristics of pessimists are (1) they believe bad events will last a long time, (2) one bad thing will spread to everything they do, and (3) they blame themselves for all their bad experiences even when it is not their fault.

Someone defined a pessimist as one who feels bad when he feels good for fear he'll feel worse when he feels better. Pessimists have simply made negative thinking a bad habit, a way of life. And that's sad.

Optimists, on the other hand, are undaunted by defeat. When they are confronted with the inevitable hard knocks of this world, they think of misfortune as opportunity. They see defeat as temporary. They limit the causes of their problem to this one case. And they seldom see defeat as their fault. Optimists faced with "evil days" (See Eph. 5:16) overcome because they "make the most of every opportunity" (TLB).

The Bible has a different word for optimism—*hope*. As it is used in the New Testament, *hope* usually refers to Christ, the Hope of this world. The apostle Paul called hope the "sure and steadfast anchor of the soul" (Heb. 6:19, NRSV) and said it will "not disappoint us" (Rom. 5:5). He also alluded to hope's being an attitude of optimism when he urged the Thessalonians to put on the helmet of hope (see 1 Thess. 5:8). Hope protects our head. It is an attitude that safeguards optimism.

Why Seek Opportunity?

Here's secret number two: **No healthy relationship can**

survive without hope. **For a relationship to grow, hope is an essential ingredient.** That's why Paul said, "Make the most of every opportunity" (Eph. 5:16, TLB). Employ hope every chance you get, because some days are downright terrible—even when you've found and are developing a relationship with the person you want to date.

"You won't believe what happened last Friday," Ron said as he walked into my office and plopped unceremoniously into a chair. "Lisa and I have been dating for a while now, and I thought things were going pretty well." He was visibly distressed. He rolled his eyes and continued, "I'm not so sure anymore."

"You're not sure about what?" I asked.

"Lisa. I'm not sure about Lisa," he said. "We had a terrible weekend. It's silly, but I misunderstood the time I was supposed to pick her up for our date on Friday, and I showed up at her house almost an hour late. Big mistake!"

"I imagine Lisa wasn't too happy about that."

"You'd better believe it," Ron snapped. "But that's not the half of it. I also forgot to make reservations at the restaurant where I promised to take her, and on top of that, I was low on cash because my paycheck was late, and I had to use most of my money to put gas in the car." He paused for a moment, shook his head, and said, "Well, to put it mildly, Lisa lost it. She blew up!"

People can be like tea bags. You never know how strong they are until you see them in hot water.

I winced inwardly as Ron told me about the rest of their date. It ended with Lisa crying and Ron bewildered. "I'm the first to admit that I'm at fault, but she whined the *entire* evening," Ron continued. "I kept waiting for her to snap out of it, but she never did. I apologized and kept trying to make up for my blunders, but she just wouldn't let go."

Every dating relationship that lasts long enough will include terrible, rotten, no-good days. It's during those bad times we learn what the person with whom we're building a relationship is grounded in—hope or despair. It is what I call "the hot-water test" of dating. As you build close relationships with others, pay attention to how they respond when things go wrong. You see, people can be like tea bags—you never know how strong they are until you see them in hot water. Do they, for the most part (we all have bad days), make the most of every opportunity? Would you consider them to be more of an optimist or a pessimist?

Finding an Optimistic Date

An old marriage and family training film depicts four different young women who each, while driving their friends to a picnic, run out of gas. Their responses are intriguing. One young woman screams at her friends and blames them for not warning her that the gas was low. Another becomes sullen and assumes the role of a victim. Another tells everyone to stand along the road with her to help flag down another car for help. Still another spreads the picnic on the grass nearby and ignores the problem, waiting for a solution to happen. The film ends by asking: Which young woman would make the best marriage partner?

Most of us would probably be happier with a date who is the "no big problem, it's just a minor inconvenience" type. Not that a date should deny reality. Glossing over real problems by ignoring them or making them seem smaller than they are is seldom a solution. Rather, the point is this: Christian hope is an essential ingredient in developing positive attitudes about life. How we react to situations is merely an indicator of our deeper thought life.

To help you identify the character of hope in the people you date, here are a few of the most important characteristics to look for.

1. *The Optimistic Date Perseveres*

Perseverance or determination is critical in every long-term, healthy relationship. Without the motivation to "hang in there," the slightest unexpected winds can easily throw a relationship off course.

Ask any salesperson. This is a profession keenly aware of rejection. The typical salesperson hears "no" 40 times to every "yes." Salespeople know that without perseverance their livelihood is doomed.

Using sales as an analogy doesn't mean you have to force every relationship to work. Some relationships aren't going to work. But those that have potential, the ones that exhibit more than a few of the qualities outlined in this book, deserve a big helping of perseverance.

Listen to what Paul says in Rom. 5:3-4 about progressing from the turbulent times to achieving hope: "We know that suffering produces perseverance; perseverance, character; and character, hope." Without sticking it out through bad days, the blessing of genuine hope doesn't have a chance of materializing in your relationship.

2. *The Optimistic Date Sees Difficulties as Temporary*

In recent years as a psychologist in a medical center, I found one of my most devastating assignments was the burn unit. In working with burn patients, I watched the healing process and saw firsthand how it can be hindered or helped by the patient's outlook. One of the bravest and most optimistic patients I ever met was Kim Holt.

Kim was a high school senior preparing to enter Northwest Nazarene College when a backyard barbecue turned deadly. Kim's boyfriend was killed in the explosion, and the accident left her with third-degree burns over most of her body. In the hospital for months, Kim endured the excruciating pain of having her arms and legs pulled, bent, and massaged to get the tendons stretched back in the right direction.

Six years after the accident I invited Kim to speak in one of my university classes. Those 75 students were breathless as she told her story. When asked what enabled her to cope, Kim said, "God helped me see this situation as temporary suffering. I have grieved a lot, but I decided it wasn't going to slow me down forever."

Optimists see difficulties—sometimes even horrendous difficulties—as temporary. Healthy individuals view difficulties as things to overcome, not things to be overwhelmed by. Whenever I am faced with a tough time that starts to color my whole world, I think of people like Kim.

3. The Optimistic Date Is Not Hurt Easily

In chapter 1 of this book, we discussed the different approaches people take to dating. The whiners were the ones who always had a good (and often whiny) excuse as to why they weren't pursuing relationships. Let's examine now the kind of person who whines no matter what—in or out of a dating relationship. Their boats are constantly being upset, and they have the part of victim down pat.

When Rob bounded into my office to talk about his date with Lisa and how she reacted to his blunders, I couldn't help but think how differently their date might have been if Lisa had not taken his perceived thoughtlessness so personally. If, for example, Lisa had adjusted to the inconvenience with an attitude that said, "Well, what matters is that we're together now—let's be creative with the time we do have," my hunch is that it could have turned into a pleasant, memorable date.

I remember a time when Leslie and I ended up going to an art museum instead of a baseball game because I was short on cash. The game would have been fun, but the museum visit was free! Leslie is a real trooper. She didn't get her feelings hurt. She didn't take the unexpected turn of events as a personal insult. She helped me turn a problem into a pleasant solution. That afternoon became a date both of us remember with warm feelings.

I remember going from room to room in the museum individually, choosing our favorite art pieces, and then seeing how our tastes in art compared. Leslie has shared that what sticks out most to her about that date was the fun we had acting like the statues and the picture taking we did. It wasn't the date we had planned. Both of us had wanted to see the Pirates, not Picasso. But it's a date we will always remember—primarily because Leslie rolled with the punches. When people operate from an optimistic standpoint, they are not easily ruffled. They know how to adjust to things beyond their control.

4. *The Optimistic Date Is Flexible*

The Chinese symbols for *crisis* and *opportunity* are the same. Literally translated, the symbol reads, "Crisis is an opportunity riding the dangerous wind." There's real value in developing an attitude that adapts to unexpected change. It's all about turning stumbling blocks into stepping-stones.

How does one become flexible when faced with stressful situations? First, view stress as normal and an important part of life. Understand that life isn't perfect. Accept the fact that things don't always go as planned.

Research has shown that people who view adversities as natural almost always adapt more quickly and are less likely to suffer depression or anxiety. In short, they are healthier people because they are flexible. Not only are these kinds of people much easier to be with than those who hit their heads against the wall when confronted with stress, but they are probably more mature as well. When building relationships, look for this sign of maturity.

If it's not there, as a friend, don't just walk away; lovingly encourage this person to develop flexibility. Keep in mind that some of us are pessimists about to become optimists. Life experiences can change a person's outlook on life. In fact, because we're hopeful in Christ, we can always know that change is possible.

5. The Optimistic Date Knows How to Dream

The musical play *Man of La Mancha* is one of my all-time favorites. It very clearly demonstrates the power of hope. In the story a crazy old man named Don Quixote, suffering from what we would now call senile psychosis, decides that he is a knight. Too bad for him that chivalry died a hundred years earlier. Still, thinking he is a knight, Don Quixote puts on a strange suit of armor and rides into the world to battle evil and protect the weak and powerless. He brings along his servant, Sancho Panza, as his squire.

The dreams and hopes of the people around us powerfully shape our lives.

When they arrive at a broken-down old inn used by mule traders, Don Quixote calls the innkeeper the lord of a great castle. In the inn he meets the most miserable human being imaginable, a pathetic orphan girl who does menial chores and is degraded by the mule traders. Don Quixote pronounces this wretched girl the great lady, Dulcinea, and begs for her handkerchief as a token to carry with him into battle.

Everyone thinks Don Quixote is bonkers, but at the end of the play the old man, who is now about to die, is no longer suffering from these delusions. In a moving scene, all the people he has renamed appear at his bedside and beg him not to change. His senile excitement about their future has transformed them, and they have become the people whom this insane visionary saw in them.

The message of the play is this: The dreams and hopes of the people around us powerfully shape our lives. If they help us dream, especially on dark days, they keep love alive. To paraphrase a proverb, "Where there is no vision, *a healthy dat-*

ing relationship will perish" (see Prov. 29:18, KJV).

People who achieve are dreamers. I have a plaque in my study with the following quote from Henry David Thoreau: "If one advances confidently in the direction of his dreams, and endeavors to live the life which he has imagined, he will meet with a success unexpected in common hours." I believe that and do my best to try to live by it. What we consciously dream about, what we envision for the future, the goals we set determine the road we travel. Worthy dreams filled with godly hope can take us to unimagined vistas.

> **What we consciously dream about, what we envision for the future, the goals we set determine the road we travel.**

Those without noble dreams are likely to flounder in self-pity and make the people in their lives miserable. The saddest statistic I know is this: 64 percent of today's teenagers believe life will be worse for them in 10 years. In other words, the majority of young people are pessimists in desperate need of hope.

Of course, it is possible to have dreams that are not godly. So how should a Christian dream? Allow me to paraphrase the words of Paul in Phil. 4:8: "Whatever is true, whatever is noble, whatever is right, whatever is pure, whatever is lovely, whatever is admirable . . . *dream on these things.*"

The focus of a healthy dream and vision is not on "laying up treasures on earth" (see Matt. 6:19, KJV), but on pleasing God. And sometimes that involves risk. Do you or the person you're interested in dating know how to take a noble risk? Are you willing to risk the rejection that often comes from not being pressured into going along with what everyone else is doing? Do you have the backbone to risk ridicule for the sake of your faith? Or do you play it safe and cautiously opt for the comfort of behaving like everyone else? It was H. C. G. Moule who rightly said, "The frontiers of the kingdom of God were never advanced by men and women of caution."

So this is my second challenge to you:
Develop a positive outlook on life.
And as you build close relationships,
seek out people who know how to dream
and work at seeing their visions
become realities.

SELF-TEST

1. **Do you enjoy listening more to depressing music or upbeat, inspiring music?**
   Depressing   *Upbeat*
   1   2   3   4   5   6   7

2. **Do you easily get your feelings hurt?**
   Often   *Never*
   1   2   3   4   5   6   7

3. **If you fail an important exam, are you more likely to say, "I'm not as smart as the other people taking the exam," or "I didn't prepare well for the exam"?**
   Not as smart   *Didn't prepare well*
   1   2   3   4   5   6   7

4. **Do you see tough times as permanent or temporary?**
   Permanent   *Temporary*
   1   2   3   4   5   6   7

5. Are you fearful or hopeful about the future?

Fearful   *Hopeful*

1	2	3	4	5	6	7

6. Do you show signs of dedication and perseverance?

Rarely   *Always*

1	2	3	4	5	6	7

Scoring

Tally the six items. There is a possible range of scores from 6 to 42. The higher the score, the more you see you or your date as being optimistic. Remember: this questionnaire is only a tool to get you thinking. Remember, too, that positive change is possible. Use this evaluation to determine your next step in pursuing hope.

Something to Think and Talk About

- If a person is not optimistic and hopeful, how do you think that would impact a dating relationship?
- Who is the most visionary, optimistic, and hopeful person you know? How would you describe that person's relationships?
- This chapter noted the following ingredients as essential to optimism: perseverance, not being easily hurt, knowing how to dream, flexibility, and the ability to see setbacks as temporary. What other qualities do you think might be a part of having a bright outlook?
- What does it mean to you to have vision for your future? How would you describe your personal vision?
- How do you usually respond when things don't go your way?

For Further Study

In some ways 1 Peter is the statement par excellence of the Christian's hope. First, this hope is rooted in Christ's resurrection (1:3). Second, the resurrection of Christ is a cause for all believers to hope (1:21). Third, such hope is the criterion of spiritual beauty (3:5). Fourth, it is also the content of Christian testimony (3:15). Study 1 Peter to discover its message of hope.

· 4 ·

A Fool for Love

*Therefore do not be foolish, but understand
what the Lord's will is.*—EPH. 5:17

HAVE YOU ever noticed how foolish people can be? Consider
the following true story.

Judge John Week spotted a man wearing a hat, sitting in
the rear of his Minneapolis courtroom. Disturbed by this disregard for courtroom decorum, Judge Week ordered the man to
leave. When the clerk called for the burglary case of George
Rogde, who had been freed on bond, Rogde couldn't be found.
"Your honor," said the prosecuting attorney, "that is the man
you ordered from the courtroom." Police are still looking for
him.

And how about the following?

A zealous art student went to a gallery and spent a bewildered hour looking over abstract modern works. She was finally attracted to a painting consisting of a black dot on a field of
white and framed in brass. "How much is this?" she asked the
gallery attendant. "That's the light switch," he told her.

"A fool," said William Thackeray, "can no more see his
own folly than he can see his ears." Ignorance sometimes
makes fools of us. We can do or say embarrassingly foolish
things. And like the otherwise perfectly intelligent judge and

45

art student, we don't see our mistakes soon enough to save us from embarrassment.

Blunders, like mistaking a light switch for a work of art, may merely bruise a person's pride. Other foolish errors, however, can be more costly. They can ruin a person's life. That is why Paul says, "Do not be foolish, but understand what the Lord's will is" (Eph. 5:17).

While we will never totally escape silly blunders, no one needs to be a fool when it comes to God's will for your life. This chapter can help you focus on avoiding the single most foolish mistake anyone can ever make—missing out on God's will.

Don't Be a Fool

At the university where I teach psychology, we have a laboratory where rats are run through a maze. Experiments are designed to learn how animals behave under different conditions. Students taking notes on clipboards passively watch as the rats make their way to the end of the maze.

I sometimes see people who feel that the One who knows the true way is just passively watching as we explore the maze of life. That is not how God works. He is not watching, clipboard in hand, to see how long it will take us to figure things out (if indeed we *do* figure them out). No, He shows us the way. God leads His people as we study the Bible, pray, and worship Him. Anyone who is not smart enough to rely on these proven strategies is, well, as Paul said in a shocking way, "foolish."

What Is God's Will?

While I was a student in seminary, Earl Lee was my pastor. Leslie and I had him over for dinner one evening, and in the course of conversation I asked how he discerned God's will for his life. "Les," he told me, "I was in Oklahoma on a missionary tour. I told the Lord I needed to know His will, and I wanted it

Callslip Request   10/26/2013 10:56:31 AM

Request date:10/25/2013 01:26 PM
Request ID: 42591
Call Number:306.73 P263
Item Barcode:

Author: Parrott, Les.
Title: 7 secrets of a healthy dating relationship
Enumeration:c.1Year:
Patron Name:Joy P Casperson
Patron Barcode:

Patron comment:

Request number:

Route to:
I-Share Library:

Library Pick Up Location:

settled. The answer I received was so quietly simple I hardly knew God had spoken." Pastor Lee then said, "His word to me was 'You have My will for today; I will take care of tomorrow.'"

God's will really is not complex. It is found in the same chapter of the letter to the Ephesians that 7 *Secrets* is based on. Chapter 5, verse 1 says, "Be imitators of God." That's it. That's what God's will is—that we be like Him. Verse 2 of the same chapter says it another way: "Live a life of love." God's will is that we imitate His love. It's that simple.

One of my favorite authors, Henri Nouwen, defines God's will as the way His love shapes our lives. "It is an active claiming of an intimate relationship with God," says Nouwen, "in the context of which we discover our deepest vocation and the desire to live that vocation to the fullest."

Too often we get bogged down in trying to figure out God's will when all He is asking is for us to be imitators of His love. The tough part, of course, arises in trying to discern how best to achieve that goal. It's important to remember that God has given us a mind and free will and expects us to exercise both. God's will is an active—not passive—process. The apostle Paul saw us as "God's fellow workers" (1 Cor. 3:9); we work with God to determine the outcome of events.

Often, when people discuss finding God's will, they use the word "discernment." Discernment is making the best decisions we can with the knowledge available, including (1) His Word, (2) the counsel of people we believe in, (3) good judgment, and (4) persistent intuition. Properly using all these resources results in true discernment—the ability to separate God's desires from distractions. It's all God asks of us. This is secret number three: **Learn to discern God's will for you.**

But even these resources can be misused. Some sincere but misguided people look into God's Word for specific answers to every conceivable question. It doesn't work that way. The Bible is not a crystal ball. I'm reminded of the absurd story of the man who married a woman named Grace because he read the verse that says, "My grace is sufficient for thee" (2 Cor. 12:9, KJV). This approach is obviously futile and ridiculous—it escapes discernment.

Theologian J. Kenneth Grider says, "God does not will every circumstance; but He does have a will in every circumstance." Discernment moves us to be more like God in specific situations. It helps us discover His will as we see and choose to follow the path where it leads.

Why Should We Learn to Discern?

Lettie Cowman tells an interesting story from African colonial history in her book *Springs in the Valley: Deep in the Jungles of Africa.* A traveler was making a long journey and hired some men to carry his heavy load. The traveler was in a great hurry, so the first day of the trek was fast and furious. The men marched for miles without resting.

> **Inner peace does not come in reaching the goal, but in finding the direction.**

But on the second morning these jungle tribesmen refused to move. For some unknown reason, they just sat and rested. The traveler who hired them asked the reason for this strange behavior and was informed that the tribesmen had gone too fast the first day and that they were now waiting for their souls to catch up.

People seeking the Lord's will respond as those wise tribesmen did. We keep in touch with our inner selves when we learn to discern what God wants in our lives. Living becomes more balanced and focused. We don't lose touch with our soul. Inner peace does not come in reaching the goal, but in finding the direction.

Taking time to discern God's will is the only productive way to live. Not only is it natural for those in God's will to be more relaxed, but also there is a spontaneous flow of "love, joy, peace, patience, kindness, goodness, faithfulness, gentleness and self-control" (Gal. 5:22-23).

No longer is there a tiring need to hide parts of ourselves from others. We don't have to be embarrassed by any of our choices. We can only learn from the consequences our choices bring. The person who has learned to discern God's will may be described by others as real, genuine, honest, and authentic.

Finding the Discerning Date

The apostle Paul concisely expressed God's will when he wrote, "Since the day we heard about you, we have not stopped praying for you and asking God to fill you with the knowledge of his will through all spiritual wisdom and understanding" (Col. 1:9). To achieve the kind of spiritual understanding Paul was talking about, a person needs to live happily with his or her limitations, that is, with an attitude described as humility or contentment.

The person who has learned to discern God's will may be described by others as real, genuine, honest, and authentic.

"A fool finds no pleasure in understanding but delights in airing his own opinions," says Prov. 18:2. Spiritual understanding cannot be achieved by merely using the vocabulary of a religious person. The spiritual quality in life comes through practicing the time-honored and proven techniques for discerning God's will, which include the disciplines of a daily quiet time (reading the Bible and praying), living in the spirit of prayer (staying in constant touch with God), learning how to worship God, and involving oneself in Christian service. Evidence of these disciplines, in fact, is the first clue that you are or have found a discerning person.

1. The Discerning Date Enjoys God's Word

I can't exaggerate the importance of building a relationship with someone who loves God's Word. Everyone seeking the Lord's will relies on the Bible to point the way. Even powerful presidents have confessed their reliance on God's Word. Teddy Roosevelt said, "The teachings of the Bible are so interwoven with our life that it would be impossible to figure what life would be if those teachings were removed."

Perhaps the best description of the Bible I have ever read came from old-time professional baseball player and evangelist Billy Sunday. He talked about entering the "wonderful temple" of the Bible:

> I entered at the portico of Genesis, walked down through the Old Testament art galleries, where pictures of Noah, Abraham, Moses, Joseph, Isaac, Jacob, and Daniel hung on the wall. I passed into the music room of Psalms, where the Spirit swept the keyboard of nature until it seemed that every reed and pipe in God's great organ responded to the tuneful harp of David, the sweet singer of Israel. I entered the chamber of Ecclesiastes, where the voice of the preacher was heard; and into the conservatory of Sharon, where the Lily of the Valley's sweet-scented spices filled and perfumed my life. I entered the business office of Proverbs, and then into the observatory room of the Prophets, where I saw telescopes of various sizes, pointed to far off events, but all concentrated upon the bright and morning star.
>
> I entered the audience room of the King of Kings, and caught a vision of His glory from the standpoint of Matthew, Mark, Luke, and John, passed into the Acts of the Apostles, where the Holy Spirit was doing His work in the formation of the infant church. Then into the correspondence room, where sat Paul, Peter, James, and John, penning their epistles. I stepped into the throne room of Revelation, where towered the glittering peaks, and got a vision of the King sitting upon the throne in all His glory, and I cried:

> *All hail the power of Jesus' name,*
> *Let angels prostrate fall,*
> *Bring forth the royal diadem,*
> *And crown Him Lord of all.*

What a picture of God's will unfolding! Each book contains stories of successes and failures, of servants and sinners.

And here's a news flash: You don't have to be a theologian to enjoy and study Scripture. Anyone who seeks the Lord's will for his or her life will find answers in the wisdom of the Bible.

Baroness Maria von Trapp was not a scholar. You may remember her life story depicted and sung in *The Sound of Music*. Maria had difficulty with formal studies. She was a free spirit. But listen to what she once wrote: "I don't remember why, but I do remember how one day when I was in my late 20s, I opened the Bible and was just amazed. I couldn't stop reading. I started in the New Testament and then went back to the Old, and there I found with growing excitement the answers to all the questions—how it all started, what is the most important thing in life. It is all there."

How well acquainted are you with the pages of God's Word? Take a peek or two. Uncover some of the most savory and unsavory characters ever written about. Share what you read with the person you're interested in dating. Make it an enjoyable time of learning and growing. Conversations about God's Word can happen over the phone, over lunch or dinner, as you walk through the mall. Learn from each other as you learn from God. And if learning God's Word doesn't appeal to the person you're interested in dating, consider why.

2. *The Discerning Date Makes Prayer a Part of Life*

For several nights, a six-year-old girl threw one shoe under her bed before going to sleep. When her mother asked why, she said, "My teacher says that if we have to kneel by our beds to look for our shoes, we'll remember to keep kneeling and say our morning prayers." I think of the grown-ups I know who struggle with consistent prayer, and somehow this shoe idea just might have merit!

Prayer brings all of us into the deepest and highest levels of the human spirit. "Prayer—secret, fervent, believing prayer —lies at the root of all personal godliness," wrote William Carey. The person following the Lord's will depends on prayer. During prayer we begin to think God's thoughts and desire the things He desires.

Some of the great giants of the faith have viewed prayer as the main business of their lives. Martin Luther declared, "I have so much business I cannot get on without spending three hours daily in prayer." John Wesley said, "God does nothing but in answer to prayer," and he backed up his conviction by devoting two hours daily to praying. And Mark tells us about Jesus' pattern of prayer: "In the morning, a great while before day, he rose and went out to a lonely place, and there he prayed" (Mark 1:35, RSV).

> **If the person you're interested in is making an effort to talk daily with God, you can be assured that he or she is learning to discern His will. We never reach out to God where He doesn't reach back.**

Not everyone will be a "great giant of the faith." Keep in mind that we all, even the prayer warriors among us, are still learning how to talk with God. Even the disciples implored Jesus, "Lord, teach us to pray" (Luke 11:1). If the person you're interested in is making an effort to talk daily with God, you can be assured that he or she is learning to discern His will. We never reach out to God where He doesn't reach back.

3. The Discerning Date Understands the Importance of Worship

Some people worship their cars. Others worship sports, music, or their wardrobes. Whatever we worship, we can be sure that each of us spends the greatest amount of time thinking about and praising the thing we consider most important in our lives. What do you worship?

I'm not saying don't enjoy cars and clothes. As long as we maintain perspective—as long as those things do not become idols and interfere with our love of God—they are things we can enjoy. Absolutely anything, though, can become a candidate for idolism—even the person you're interested in dating. God made clear in the Ten Commandments His hatred for all idolatries: "You shall have no other gods before me" (Exod. 20:3).

When you're building a close relationship, look to see what is most important in that person's life. If he or she worships God above all else, his or her life will be punctuated with praise, thanksgiving, and adoration. I like C. S. Lewis's definition of praise and worship: "Inner health made audible." Look for someone who makes worship of God a regular part of his or her life.

By the way, worship is not confined to church sanctuaries. It can occur anywhere. Brother Lawrence worshiped God in the kitchen while washing dishes. He couldn't imagine how God's people could survive without worshiping Him.

Jesus answered for all time the question on the focus of worship: "Worship the Lord your God, and serve him only" (Matt. 4:10).

4. The Discerning Date Knows How to Serve

Mark Twain said, "Let us so live that when we come to die, even the undertaker will be sorry." Not bad advice. Are you the kind of person whose absence would create the same response from the undertaker?

When Jesus gathered His disciples for the Last Supper, they were deciding among themselves who was the greatest among them (Luke 22:24). And whenever there is trouble over who is the greatest, there's bound to be trouble over who is the least. The disciples were keenly aware that there were several dirty feet needing a bath. *Someone* was going to have to wash all those dirty feet.

It was a practical custom in their culture. The people who washed feet were not as important as those whose feet were washed. So lacking the assistance of slaves, there they sat, feet caked with dirt, waiting for someone to wash them. It seemed to be a sore point. The disciples could not even talk about it rationally. No one wanted to be considered the least among the Twelve.

Jesus took a towel and basin, washed their feet, and in the process redefined greatness. "Now that I, your Lord and Teacher, have washed your feet," he told them afterward, "you also should wash one another's feet. I have set you an example that you should do as I have done for you" (John 13:14-15). Jesus calls us to seek the Lord's will by serving others in the mundane, ordinary, trivial moments of daily living.

What impact have you made on the lives of those around you? After you've examined your own life, look at the person you're interested in dating. Does he or she practice some practical form of Christian service?

A word of caution: God is not looking for self-righteous servants. Self-righteous servants are those who want to look like Christian servants without actually being such. These false servants pick and choose where they'll serve instead of meeting the needs God brings to their attention. Self-righteousness is the result of calculating and scheming to look like a servant as a way (supposedly) to earn points with God.

True service, on the other hand, is a response to God's whispered promptings and divine urges. Someone who is a true servant humbly helps others without concern for recognition or reward. True servants may, for example, give someone a ride even when it is not convenient, send a card to a person who is sick, clean up a disorganized Sunday School room, loan a book, go out of their way to talk with someone who is lonely, and so on.

Are you a true servant? When building a relationship with someone, consider the person's motives and life of service. Is that person serving God or self?

5. *The Discerning Date Makes You More Like Christ*

The final quality I want to mention regarding the person who is seeking the Lord's will is perhaps the most telling. More than any other quality, it can reveal whether a person is seriously seeking the Lord's will.

The ultimate test of a relationship is whether, by the quality of a person's inner life, each calls the other to a deeper relationship with Christ. Ps. 42:7 reads, "Deep calls to deep." Do you catch glimpses in each other of a deeper walk with Him, hints of something more than you now know in your relationships with God? Do you each want to launch deeper in your relationship with Him? Are you both on a quest to live out God's love in your lives? Are you lifting each other up or pulling each other down?

If, when you are around this person, you do not find that you are growing closer to God in your relationship, chances are this person is not serious about knowing God. Look for a person who helps you be more like Christ.

So this is my third challenge to you: Develop a dialogue with God to discover His will for you. Then, as you build close relationships, look for those who seek God's will.

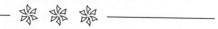

SELF-TEST

1. **Do you routinely read and study the Bible?**   Yes   No

2. **Is consistent prayer a part of your life?**   Yes   No

3. **Do you have quiet times with God?**   Yes   No

4. **Do you enjoy worshiping God?**   Yes   No

5. **Are you willing to lend a hand without recognition?**   Yes   No

6. **Would you say your behavior is Christlike when you are with your date?**   Yes   No

Scoring

Out of these half-dozen questions, how many times were you able to circle "Yes"? The more questions you answered yes to, the more likely it is that you are seeking the Lord's will.

Something to Think and Talk About

- Have you ever felt like a fool? Everyone has. If you are in a group discussion, take a moment to share one of your most foolish moments.
- What is the difference between a foolish moment and a foolish choice?
- William James said, "When you have to make a choice and don't make it, that in itself is a choice." What do you think he means by that? Do you have any example of how not making a choice is a choice?
- Review this chapter for a moment to make sure you understand what God's will is. Why would Earl Lee say that, regarding God's will, the answer he received was so quietly simple he hardly knew God had spoken?
- In your own experience, what spiritual discipline has helped you understand God's will best?

- In a dating relationship, how important do you think it is that the couple seek God's will together? How would they do that?

For Further Study

"Train yourself in godliness," Paul wrote to young Timothy. "For while bodily training is of some value, godliness is of value in every way" (1 Tim. 4:7-8, RSV). Paul often employed the terminology of athletics to teach that living in God's will requires effort and practice. Study 1 Cor. 9:24-27 and 2 Tim. 4:7-10. What do these passages have to say about practicing spiritual disciplines and finding God's will?

· 5 ·

Party Animals

Do not get drunk on wine, which leads to debauchery. Instead, be filled with the Spirit.—EPH. 5:18

TIM LOVED MARSHA—or at least he loved the *idea* of being in love with Marsha. The two of them met at a high school football game and soon began dating. They lived across town from one another, and both were active in their respective church youth groups. Going to different high schools and different churches required special effort to make the relationship work. Eventually, however, Tim and Marsha were together almost every Friday or Saturday evening. They talked on the phone more than their parents wished. And Marsha, a genuine romantic, often sent Tim a small gift or a card during the week.

From all appearances, things were going well. But sometime during their fourth or fifth month of dating, Marsha began questioning her feelings for Tim. "I think he's cute and all, but something doesn't feel right," she told me.

Eventually Marsha broke up with Tim. And after listening to her describe their relationship, I wasn't surprised. Marsha described how Tim's primary concern was feeling good about himself. He was more concerned with *feeling* and *looking* good

> **Knowingly or unknowingly, party animals use their dates to feel better about themselves—to get their own needs met—not to cultivate a meaningful relationship.**

than with *being* good. "With Tim, I felt more like a hood ornament than a date," Marsha confessed. "All that mattered to Tim was that he got what he wanted. If I didn't wear the right thing or say the right thing, he would sulk. I couldn't take it anymore."

A couple of weeks after Marsha's decision to break off the relationship, she showed up in my office to give me an update. "I feel so relieved," she said. "I miss being with Tim sometimes, but then I remember how I felt when we were together."

Do you know anyone like Tim? There are plenty of dating partners who are more in love with the *idea* of love than they are with the commitment of actually loving a person. I call these kinds of people "party animals" because they like the party more than the person. Often the relationship isn't important to them. What matters most to them is whether they are having fun. So they go from one "party" experience to the next, seeking their fun. They cruise from event to event and from relationship to relationship.

Knowingly or unknowingly, party animals use their dates to feel better about themselves—to get their own needs met—not to cultivate a meaningful relationship. Their unspoken, consuming question to their crowd is "How am I doing?" Their date becomes an accessory, like jewelry.

Dating, for these people, is based on externals (what the person looks like, his or her accomplishments, his or her friends) instead of internals (who the person is inside, his or her personality, hopes, dreams). They like how dating looks on them. They try on different partners similar to the way they try on new fashions. Some may even date simply because every-

> **No person, no matter how great, can consistently meet another person's needs and make him or her happy all the time. People must have their ultimate needs met in relationship with God.**

one else is dating. They feel a need to have someone by their side to feel a part of the group. To these people, whichever kind of guy or girl is in style is the kind to date. The actual person means nothing in these kinds of situations.

These are some hard truths about why some people date, but maybe the hardest truth of all is that any dating relationship based on externals is doomed to misery and failure. Why? Because no person, no matter how great, can consistently meet another person's needs and make him or her happy all the time. People must have their ultimate needs met in relationship with God. Only then are they equipped to be in a dating relationship.

What Is an Internal Orientation, and How Do I Get One?

Monty is one of my best friends. We went to school together. And even though we live across the country from each other now, we still make an effort to keep our relationship alive. I like being with Monty because we always have fun. It doesn't matter what we do or where we go—Monty makes his own party.

In fact, one of the things I appreciate most about him is that he doesn't depend on externals for happiness. Monty has a saying: "The party is where I am." Just reading that here makes it sound a little cocky, but for Monty it's not. When he says it, he actually means, "I don't have to be accepted by this group of people to have a good time," or "I don't have to give in to this pressure to have fun. I make my own party!"

Unlike Monty, party animals with an external orientation require a partylike atmosphere to be happy. This often means they give in to social pressures that go against their established moral values. They compromise themselves for the sake of what others have designated as fun.

Let me relate the idea of an internal orientation to dating relationships. Remember the story of Cinderella? Around the globe the story has been told of this stepdaughter, forced to toil as an ignoble servant to her wicked stepfamily. Long story short: She gets to go to the ball (that is, the party). She meets a handsome and gallant Prince Charming. They fall in love. He takes her away, and they "live happily ever after."

All of us who heard that story as a child probably thought Cinderella, after having worked so hard for those wicked "steps," deserved to have the prince cart her away from it all. It never enters the mind of a child that the two of them hardly know each other. That's fairy-tale love!

This is the point. Some people operate from the view that life should be like Cinderella's story. Their unconscious mind won't accept reality. They treat fiction as fact. Deep down, they long for a Prince Charming or Cinderella to turn their world inside out and make everything bad go away. They long for a "party" to make everything happy forever, even in the face of reality—a reality that tells us worthwhile relationships take time and energy to cultivate.

Robert Runcie, archbishop of Canterbury, gave a marvelous homily at the wedding of Prince Charles and Lady Diana. And while the current state of that royal union is in a shambles, what he said that day still has merit. He said,

> Here is the stuff of which fairy tales are made, the prince and princess on their wedding day. But fairy tales usually end at this point with the simple phrase, "They lived happily ever after." This may be because fairy tales regard marriage as an anticlimax after the romance of courtship. This is not the Christian view. Our faith sees the wedding day as the place where the real adventure begins. The same could be said of the initial stages of building re-

lationships. People with an internal orientation aren't looking for someone to meet all their needs. They don't depend on their date to make their life a party. They know the difference between fairy tales and real life. They know that while it's fun, even dating has its disappointments. No one person can meet all our needs. Those with an internal orientation know that only God can ultimately meet their needs.

Whenever I talk to dating couples about having an internal orientation, they eventually ask how they can acquire it. Fortunately I can point them to the answer given long ago by Paul when he said, "Do not get drunk on wine, which leads to debauchery. Instead, be filled with the Spirit" (Eph. 5:18). In other words, avoid the temporary party. Look for and find the *lasting* one, the one that fills not just for a short time, but forever. That is the only way I know for not falling into the fairy tale trap of depending on externals.

This is secret number four: **Be spiritually-minded, filled with the Holy Spirit.**

Why Have an Internal Orientation?

The old saying "Opposites attract" is based on the phenomenon that many individuals are drawn to people who complement themselves—who have skills they do not, who complete them in some way they cannot do for themselves. Even Proverbs says, "As iron sharpens iron, so one man sharpens another" (27:17). Our incompleteness and differences provide us sharpening power.

While God didn't create dating (in fact, you'll not find one verse on the subject in His Word), He does have more than a little to say about building relationships. Relationship building is God giving us the opportunity to improve who and what we are while offering us a chance to give to others. It is not a way for us to make up for who and what we are not. Everyone has rough edges needing to be honed, and while a dating relationship can sharpen our character, it cannot make up for who we aren't.

A healthy dating relationship challenges us to new heights and calls each to be the best person possible. But *no* dating partner, no matter how wonderful, can magically make us whole. People who believe the myth that their dating partner can make them whole become dependent on their partner in a way that, by all psychological and spiritual standards, is unhealthy. If the relationship lasts, partners cultivate a reliance for unrealistic support and assurance that generates a strong sense of inferiority.

In short, codependent partners become very shallow people—what I call "party people." Paul said to these types, "You are looking only on the surface of things" (2 Cor. 10:7). That is the fate of the external orientation. It focuses only on the glossy exterior and never plunges to meaningful depths.

An internal orientation, on the other hand, allows us to find fuller meaning in life. It prevents us from being tossed about by every wind that blows (see Eph. 4:14). It anchors our being in the knowledge that "the God of peace will be with" us (Phil. 4:9). When a person has God in his or her life, he or she does not rely on another person for fulfillment. Let me say it again: *No human being can meet all of another person's needs all of the time.*

Finding the Spirit-filled Date

So just how can you tell if someone is a Spirit-filled person? There's no test you can give. The person won't walk up and tell you he or she is Spirit-filled. (And if that person does, chances are he or she isn't!)

There's no easy way to get a glimpse of someone's inner being. We have to rely on what we can see to guide us. Here are some characteristics Spirit-filled people may exhibit: (1) they are aware God is at work in their lives; (2) they have a growing passion to know God better; and (3) they know God cares for them, and they trust Him with their problems. Let's look at these three characteristics in depth.

1. The Spirit-filled Date Knows God

A young man who was desperately seeking God sought out a wise old man who lived in a nearby beach house and posed the question: "Old man, how can I know God?" The old man, who knew God at a depth few of us experience, pondered the question for a very long time. At last he responded quietly: "Young man, I am not sure I can help you—for you see, I have a very different problem. I cannot *not* know Him."

Sometimes people limit their vision of God. Like flies crawling across the roof of the Sistine Chapel, they are unable to see the beauty and grandeur at their feet. They are blind to God's handiwork. They are looking for God "out there" somewhere and missing His everyday nearness. Spirit-filled people, however, see God working in their lives every day. They do not fall into the trap of believing that God speaks only through miracles, for example. They see God in the ordinary events of life.

Gerhard Frost puts it this way: "I believe the small moment is the carrier of God's most endearing gift, and that it must not be permitted to slip away unsavored and unappreciated."

2. The Spirit-filled Date Has a Passion for God

Bart Starr, former quarterback of the world champion Green Bay Packers, said something interesting about his coach, Vince Lombardi: "He taught me that you can't win without a flaming desire to win. Winning has got to dominate all your waking hours. It can't ever wane. It's got to glow in you all the time."

I remember when I committed myself to a passion for God. I was a sophomore in college. All my life I had grown up in the church. I had committed my life to Jesus when I was very young. As I grew older, it sometimes felt I was going through the motions, as if my faith were more my parents' than my own. That's when I decided I wanted a passionate faith—a flaming desire to live for God. It was a real turning point in my life.

Not long after making that decision, I bought a painting of a deer in the woods. In the corner of the painting are these words: "As a hart longs for flowing streams, so longs my soul for thee, O God" (Ps. 42:1, RSV). Many years later, that same painting hangs in my office as a constant reminder to my decision to be passionate about God.

Not everyone you meet will have such visible evidence of commitment to God, but that individual's passion for Him will definitely be easy to detect. It will affect every area of his or her life. Look for this kind of person.

3. The Spirit-filled Date Turns Worry over to God

A University of Michigan study determined 60 percent of human fears are totally unwarranted; 20 percent, while probably legitimate, are past activities and are completely beyond our control; and another 10 percent are so petty they don't make much difference at all. Of the remaining 10 percent of our worries and fears, only 4 to 5 percent are really justifiable. And even half of this residue of viable fears is beyond our capacity to change! The final half, or 2 percent, of our worries that are justifiable can be solved easily, according to researchers, "if we stop stewing and start doing!" I can't vouch for these statistics, but they make a point. Most worries are not worth the chatter they generate.

The apostle Paul would not be surprised by these contemporary findings. Long ago he wrote to young churches to stop perpetually worrying (Phil. 4:6). But he didn't stop there. He also gave us a prescription for worry: We are to bring our requests to God, with an attitude of thanksgiving, expecting what awaits us is "the peace of God, which transcends all understanding" (vv. 6-7).

The kind of person you want to become and the kind you want to date is the kind who has learned to sift through the minutiae of life and focus on what really matters—to "stop stewing and start doing!" It's not always an easy task, but the apostle Peter reminds us why we should do it. He says to "cast all your anxiety on him because he cares for you" (1 Pet. 5:7). Turning our worry over to God can leave us free to enjoy the *real* "party"—the party of life.

Clue In to the Party of Life

OK, so now you're concentrating on your own internal orientation that is built on a life centered on God, and you're looking for a dating partner who is doing the same. Your chances for building a meaningful and happy relationship have increased exponentially. The internally oriented person is very special. He or she celebrates life, not the occasion. This person doesn't have to look for a party to be happy. For this individual, *life* is the party! Do yourself a favor: be and date a *true* party animal.

So this is my fourth challenge to you: Continually base your happiness on God, and never depend on an external party for your happiness. Then, as you build close relationships, look for those who look to God to meet their ultimate needs.

SELF-TEST

1. Do you appreciate the people you date more for who they are or for whether they can make you look good? In other words, do you think they feel more like a person or an accessory when you are together?

Person   Accessory
1   2   3   4   5   6   7

2. Do you use your date to get your needs met? Do you disregard his or her feelings or wishes? Do you respect your date? In other words, does your date feel more cared for or used by you?

Cared for   Used
1   2   3   4   5   6   7

3. Do you depend on external factors for your personal happiness? For example, do you depend on buying new things to feel good? Do you rely on your date to make you feel better? Do you depend on internal factors to bring you happiness? Do you rely on God's Holy Spirit to meet your ultimate needs? Which is it, more internal or external?

Internal   External
1   2   3   4   5   6   7

4. Does being around you challenge your date to go deeper in his or her relationship with God? Or does time spent with you move your date to focus more on superficial, surface issues?

Deeper   Surface
1   2   3   4   5   6   7

Scoring

Tally your score. Scores may range from 4 to 28. The higher your score, the more likely it is that you have an external orientation than an internal orientation. Remember: this questionnaire is only a tool to get you thinking.

Something to Think and Talk About

- What do you think about Tim and Marsha's relationship? Do you think Marsha did the right thing to break off the relationship with Tim? Why? What would you have done differently?
- In your own words, what does it mean to have an internal orientation? You may want to review the chapter, but try to define this concept in your own words. How would you explain its importance to a dating relationship?
- Remember Monty's phrase "The party is where I am"? Can you think of circumstances in which you might use it—even in saying it to yourself—that would help you cultivate an internal orientation? What are the circumstances, and how would you use the phrase?
- One of the main points of this chapter is that no human being can meet another person's needs all of the time. What do you think of that? Why is that true? And with that being true, where do we get our needs met?
- Paul urges us to be filled with the Spirit. What can people do to become filled with God's Holy Spirit? What is the danger of dating someone who is not Spirit-filled?
- Do you know any *true* party animals—the kind of persons who not only have fun but also understand the purpose for their celebration? Who are they, and what about them do you appreciate or admire? Do you look for these qualities in a dating partner?

For Further Study

Review this chapter by circling every reference to Scripture. Next, write each reference on a sheet of paper, and then look each one up in your Bible. For each verse or passage, ask yourself what it has to say about finding true love.

· 6 ·

Making Music

Speak to one another with psalms, hymns and spiritual songs. Sing and make music in your heart to the Lord.—EPH. 5:19

"A BIRD DOESN'T sing because he has an answer—he sings because he has a song," said Joan Anglund. Do you know people who, while they may have all the answers, don't have a song? I'm not talking about people who aren't musical. I'm talking about people without joy. These people didn't set out to be unhappy. They didn't plan to be unhappy. They became unhappy by default.

Let me tell you what I mean. I always thought we had two options when circumstances didn't go our way: the decision to be happy despite our situation or the decision to be unhappy. However, after studying these choices for several years now, I have concluded that if we fail to make the positive choice to be happy, then unhappiness can move in without invitation. If we don't choose to be happy, unhappiness can result by default.

My dad is one of the happiest people I know. My mom says he thinks every day is Christmas. Even when times are tough, he maintains a positive attitude. Many times while I was growing up, he said, "Les, you can choose to be happy— happiness is a habit you cultivate. It's your option."

I never fully understood what Dad meant by happiness being a choice until I came across some research in a class I was teaching. My wife, Leslie, and I team-teach a course on marriage and family therapy at our university. We have used various textbooks, but there is one book that is perhaps more popular than all the others combined. In this highly respected and widely used textbook, *Building a Successful Marriage* (Landis and Landis), written in the usual formal format for college study, there is just one italicized sentence: *"The most important characteristic of a marriageable person is the habit of happiness."* Research has found that the person who is upbeat and positive, who chooses to be happy regardless of his or her circumstances, who can make music in his or her heart, is usually an above-average risk for a lifelong, fulfilling marriage partner.

> **If we fail to make the positive choice to be happy, then unhappiness can move in without invitation.**

Happiness, in many ways, is what the good news of Jesus Christ is all about. "Good news" by definition cannot be gloomy. Samuel Shoemaker said, "The surest mark of a Christian is not faith, or even love, but joy." Sir Thomas Taylor said, "You cannot read the Gospels without seeing that Jesus did not tell men how to be good in the manner of the moralists of every age; He told them how to be happy."

Jesus practiced this kind of deep happiness. He believed everyone should make happiness a habit. When He taught the disciples (on whose shoulders He would lay the full responsibility for spreading the gospel), His first lesson to them revolved around how to be happy even when times are tough. He began His "Sermon on the Mount" this way:

Happy are those who know they are spiritually poor . . . Happy are those who mourn . . . Happy are those who are humble . . . Happy are those whose greatest desire is to do what God requires . . . Happy are those who are merciful to others . . . *Happy* are the pure in heart . . . *Happy* are those who work for peace . . . *Happy* are those who are persecuted because they do what God requires . . . *Happy* are you when people insult you and persecute you and tell all kinds of evil lies against you because you are my followers. Be happy and glad *(Matt. 5:3-12, TEV)*.

And Jesus did not just preach a message of joy; He lived it.

On the eve of His crucifixion, Jesus said to His disciples: "These things I have spoken to you, that my *joy* may be in you, and that your *joy* may be full" (John 15:11, RSV, emphasis added). In the days ahead, Jesus would show them firsthand how to choose a spirit of joy in the face of adversity, affliction, and even death. He prepared them for the time when He would be gone from them in body (Matt. 5:11-12). Jesus was "a man of sorrows and acquainted with grief" (Isa. 53:3, NKJV), yet He possessed a deep joy beyond anything the world could match. It's a joy still springing from God's love. And Jesus offers that same joy to His followers (John 15:11; Ps. 16:11).

Happiness vs. Joy

The word *happiness* comes from the same root as the word *happening*. It suggests that happiness is based on something happening to us. Happiness can be circumstantial. If I get an A on a test, I'm happy. If I get a new CD, I'm happy. If my friends say nice things, I'm happy. But this kind of circumstantial happiness is not what we're after.

Circumstantial happiness lasts only while circumstances go our way. Unfortunately, circumstances are unpredictable. They can change as quickly as the wind, and when they do, happiness loses its guarantee.

Joy (deep happiness), the way Jesus defines it, is something that defies circumstances and occurs in spite of difficult situations. Whereas happiness is a circumstance-based feeling, joy is a life-permeating attitude. Joy can be gained through a choice. As Paul Sailhamer says, "Joy is that deep, settled confidence that God is in control of every area of my life."

Is it really possible to be joyful when things aren't going well? Whenever that question pops into my head, I turn to a small letter in the New Testament called Philippians. It was written by the apostle Paul when he was a prisoner in Rome. He sent it to his fellow Christians in Philippi. In it he disclosed the secret of Christian joy. At least 19 times in four chapters, Paul mentions joy, rejoicing, or gladness.

The letter is all the more striking because Paul wrote it in a Roman jail cell. What possible reason could he have had to be joyful? He was in prison! Yet in spite of his danger and discomfort, Paul's heart overflowed with joy. His secret is found in another word often repeated in Philippians: the word *mind*. As humans, we have minds equipped with the capacity to think. Paul tells us that the secret of joy when things aren't going well is found in the way we think—our attitude.

A growing relationship with Jesus transforms our mind (Rom. 12:2), and joy is the by-product. When Paul listed the fruit of the Spirit in Galatians 5, he included joy. It's the outgrowth of a love relationship with Christ. It is this relationship with Christ that allows us to face the challenges of our lives with joy. Christ, more than others, knew how to do that. "For the joy set before him [he] endured the cross" (Heb. 12:2).

This is secret number five: **Seek the genuine joy that God gives.**

Why Seek Joy?

Tim Hansel knows pain. He has lived for years with continual physical pain and writes about it in *You Gotta Keep Dancin'*. His pain is the result of a climbing mishap in the Sierra Mountains. Tim and two mountaineering friends were crossing over a crevasse in a snow glacier when Tim slipped and fell over the edge. He landed on the ice many feet below. He was fortunate to have survived but has lived with intense pain ever since. His response to the pain? He says, "Pain is inevitable, but misery is optional."

How can someone with chronic pain say that? Tim says misery is optional, because he has a joy that comes from his relationship with Christ: "God has given us such immense freedom that He will allow us to be as miserable as we want to be," says Tim.

He's right. I know people who spend their entire lives without joy. They have chosen to be pulled into the trap of endlessly putting off joy. They assign a weak hybrid of joy as a reward to achievement—when I get a car or when I get out on my own. The problem with this thinking is they are still depending on circumstances for their joy. They never access the joy available every day to each of us.

Why seek joy? Because life isn't easy. That's a promise. Life is difficult. Jesus reminds us that in this world there will be trouble. But He says we are not merely to endure these tough times. We are to "be of good cheer," for Christ has "overcome the world" (John 16:33, KJV).

There is another reason for seeking joy—it's our purpose. We were not created to be gloomy or depressed. God never intended it. One of my favorite professors, Lewis Smedes, used to say, "You and I were created for joy, and if we miss it, we miss the reason for our existence."

Finding a Joyful Date

Abraham Lincoln said, "Most people are about as happy as they make up their minds to be." That's the truth. People choose to be happy, and when they make it a habit, it becomes joy. As you examine your dating relationships, I can't urge you strongly enough to look for a dating partner who is joyful. In particular, ask yourself whether he or she is positive, content, and adjustable.

1. The Joyful Date Looks at Life Through a Positive Lens

One beautiful sunny day a visitor from the city was walking down a country road when he saw a farmer leaning against the fence in front of his barn. Thinking he would display his city friendliness, he walked over to the farmer and said, "Nice day, isn't it? Must be good for the corn!"

"Yes," replied the farmer, "but it's bad for the potatoes." Nothing more was said.

The following day was dark with thick, threatening clouds overhead. The friendly visitor again walked over to the farmer and said, "Nice day, isn't it? Must be good for the potatoes."

"Yes," replied the farmer, "but it's bad for the corn!"

Many people go through life like this poor farmer, always focusing on the negative side of things. Everything we put into our mental computer comes from one of five sources: hearing, seeing, smelling, tasting, or touching. Just before we put any sensory data into our computer, we exercise a God-given authority to stamp it with a bold imprint that says "positive" or another bold imprint that says "negative." Then we store the sensation in our brain, and it permanently stays there. This is why first impressions are often lasting impressions. We do not wipe out the memory of experiences; we only cover them with new memories of later sensations.

By the time each of us has reached adult years, we have developed a lifetime habit of programming our mind to be negative or positive. Two people look at the sunset; one talks about allergies, and the other talks about beauty. Nothing is so fulfilling in dating as to be with someone who has programmed himself or herself with positive attitudes to generate pleasant experiences for all the years to come—whether it is sunny or cloudy.

2. *The Joyful Date Is Content*

On graduation from college I wanted a new car. But Leslie and I had just gotten married, had started graduate school, and simply didn't have the funds. We made barely enough to buy groceries. So we made do with an old Ford pickup truck. It wasn't glamorous, but it was dependable.

One day another newly married couple living in our apartment building pulled into the parking lot with a brand-new, red sports car. It was beautiful! I couldn't believe my eyes. This machine was fully equipped with power everything. It even had leather seats. And there it sat, next to our old gray pickup.

I became unhappy every time I looked at that new car. And to think, they received this shiny automobile as a present from their wealthy parents! Here I was sweating it out in an old gray pickup without air conditioning while they were adjusting the climate control and sitting in their leather seats. It really began to bother me. I remember saying to myself, "Why do other people get all the good stuff?"

Have you ever felt that way? If you have, you know what a joy-robber envy is. But I have good news. I learned a way to avoid the pain of discontentment. After stewing for months about how others seemed to have it easier than we did, a truth dawned on me: I will never be happy unless I accept the responsibility for getting my eyes off what other people accomplish or possess. It is one of the keys to maintaining enduring joy. Whenever we begin to measure our own value and our own fulfillment by what others have or do, we are destined for depression.

I will never be happy unless I accept the responsibility for getting my eyes off what other people accomplish or possess.

Allen Parducci, a prominent University of California at Los Angeles researcher who specializes in the study of happiness, reports that money, success, health, beauty, intelligence, or power do not necessarily produce a happy life. Instead, the level of a person's joy is determined largely by whether the person compares himself or herself with other people whose circumstances are better or worse than his or her own.

Scripture says, "Keep your lives free from the love of money and be content with what you have, because God has said, 'Never will I leave you; never will I forsake you'" (Heb. 13:5). When you're building relationships, look for signs that the individual has worked at, or is working at, being content. It's no fun being around someone who measures his or her happiness by what others do or have.

3. The Joyful Date Is Adjustable

We've established that joy rests heavily on a person's ability to adjust to things beyond his or her control. Most negative people feel they could be positive if they went to a different school, had a different job, had a different set of friends, lived in a better place, had a different teacher, or even had a different set of parents. But joy doesn't always come with a new situation. As we go into new situations, we can bring the same old attitudes with us. The key is determining that your attitude will be one shaped by joy.

The most powerful example of this kind of attitude I know of is Viktor Frankl. He was a 26-year-old Jewish psychiatrist in Vienna, Austria, when he was arrested by Hitler's Gestapo and placed in a concentration camp. Month in and month out, he worked under the great smokestacks that belched out black carbon monoxide from the incinerators where his father, mother, sister, and wife had been cremated.

Each day Viktor hoped for the favor of a line server who would dip down into the broth a little deeper to come up with a few slivers of carrots or peas in his daily bowl of soup. The soup plus a thick piece of black bread made up the monotonous daily menu. In cold weather he got up an hour earlier than usual to use the burlap and wire he had scrounged to wrap his feet and legs against the crippling cold of an East European winter. His good shoes and warm socks had long since been appropriated by the guards.

When Viktor was finally interrogated, he stood naked in the center of a powerful white light illuminating a small, well-defined circle of concrete, while men in shiny boots strode to and fro in the darkened shadows. For hours, questions and accusations were shot at him by men with strident voices. They tried to break him down with every accusing lie they could conjure. Already they had taken his precious manuscript, his clothes, his wedding ring, and everything else of material value. But in the midst of this barrage of questions, an idea flashed across the mind of this young man, giving him strength and an invincible confidence. He said to himself, in a flash of spiritual insight, "They have taken from me everything I have except the power to choose my own attitudes."

Thankfully, most people are not required to cope with such devastating circumstances as the Jews faced in Nazi Germany. But the same principle that helped Viktor Frankl survive the death camps—adjusting to things beyond his control—applies to every difficult circumstance wherever and whenever it occurs.

There are many things that happen to us in life over which we have no control. Scripture tells us not to be too confident about the future, because we "do not know what a day may bring forth" (Prov. 27:1). Look for someone who understands and accepts this as part of life, choosing to be happy even when things don't go as planned.

The Power of Attitudes

The people of the world could be divided into two camps when it comes to attitudes: those filled with enduring joy in spite of their circumstances and those depending on their circumstances to bring them happiness. By force of habit, each of us is either basically positive or basically negative. The negative person defends his or her attitude with the rationale of being realistic, while the positive person looks beyond the current state of affairs and sees people and situations in terms of possibilities. If the person you're interested in dating is described by the latter, your chances for building a healthy relationship increase substantially.

So this is my fifth challenge to you: When building close relationships, pray for God's deep joy for those for whom you're learning to care. And, too, ask God to share His joy with you.

SELF-TEST

Can you be happy even when things don't go your way?
1. _____ Almost never
2. _____ Every once in a while
3. _____ Some of the time
4. _____ Almost always

Would you say you have a positive attitude?
1. _____ Not at all. I'm negative about most things.
2. _____ Yes! But I'm too positive, never really in touch with reality.
3. _____ I'm positive about most things.
4. _____ I usually have a positive attitude even in tough times.

Is your attitude influenced by what others have or do?
1. _____ Yes. I'm obsessed with others' possessions.
2. _____ Sometimes. I try not to be envious but often am.
3. _____ Yes, but I'm sometimes saddened by things others can't do or have.
4. _____ My happiness is almost never affected by what others have.

Do you adjust to things beyond your control?
1. _____ Not at all. A little rain can ruin my whole day.
2. _____ Rarely. I don't like unfortunate surprises and it shows.
3. _____ I am adjustable in most circumstances even when things get bad.
4. _____ I am very adjustable and can be content even when things don't go as planned.

Scoring

Tally the four items. There is a possible range of scores from 4 to 16. The higher the score, the more you see yourself as being joyful. Of course, joy could never be reduced to a number, so remember to use this questionnaire only as a tool to get you thinking.

Something to Think and Talk About

- How would you define happiness? How is it different from joy?
- What do you think is meant by the statement "Pain is inevitable, but misery is optional"? Do you have any examples of what this means in your own life?
- Why do you think joy is an important quality to look for in a dating partner?
- Jesus talked a lot about joy. How did He practice what He preached?
- This chapter pointed out three of the most important qualities of a joyful person—positive outlook, content-

ment, adjustability. What other qualities do you feel contribute to being genuinely joyful?

For Further Study

Study the letter to the Philippians. It has a lot to say about joy. Take a red pen and circle the words "joy" and "rejoice" each time they appear in these four chapters. Then take a blue pen and circle the words "mind" and "think." What are the secrets this letter reveals about being a joyful person?

·7·

The Attitude of Gratitude

Always giving thanks to God the Father for everything, in the name of our Lord Jesus Christ.—EPH. 5:20

OF ALL THE seasons, autumn is my favorite. There's a distinct aura surrounding it. Leaves become brilliant. Mornings are crisp and frosty. Firewood is cut. Footballs are thrown. Pumpkins grow big. And of course, school begins. You may think it's goofy, but I love school. Freshly sharpened pencils. A clean stack of notebook paper. The cracking spine of a new textbook. Autumn always signifies a fresh start for me. Labor Day is my New Year's Day.

The main reason I enjoy autumn, however, is that Thanksgiving is my favorite holiday. Thanksgiving doesn't have the same kind of commercial hype that surrounds Christmas. The emphasis is not on shopping. It's on home and family. And food—homemade rolls, sweet potatoes, corn bread dressing, pumpkin pie, and, of course, a turkey! Thanksgiving is also a time for reflection. It's an annual reminder of God's faithfulness. It is a time when we set aside our self-seeking ways, and the majesty of simple things is brought to mind. The meal, the football games, and the family gatherings encourage a sincere spirit of gratitude.

The Roman philosopher Cicero said, "Gratitude is not only the greatest of virtues, but the parent of all the others." It seems that if a person is routinely grateful—with an attitude of gratitude—he or she becomes a better person.

I'm not talking about saying "Thank you" upon receiving a compliment or a birthday present. That's common courtesy or politeness. I'm talking about gratitude that permeates a person's being, not only politely expressed but also deeply experienced. I know an 84-year-old man who has what I'm talking about. He once told me, "When I wake up in the morning, I lie there for a moment, and then I wiggle my toes. If they move, then I say, 'Thank You, Lord, for one more day of life.'" It reminds me of G. K. Chesterton's short poem, "Evening," which is really a bedtime prayer:

> Here dies another day
> during which I have had eyes, ears, hands,
> and the great world round me;
> and with tomorrow begins another.
> Why am I allowed two?

A genuinely grateful person is in awe of the gift of life. Going beyond the civilities of "please" and "thank you," he or she is grateful for each new day of life. From the time they awake until the time they go to sleep at night, grateful people exude a contagious appreciation for life. Each day is precious. Forgive me if I point out the obvious, but gratitude makes these people easy to live with.

I'm not sure where I first heard that catchy phrase—"the attitude of gratitude"—maybe from someone on an audiotape, or perhaps it was on a bumper sticker. Wherever or whenever really doesn't matter. All I know is that thankfulness really is the parent of all other virtues.

What Is "the Attitude of Gratitude"?

To understand what it means to be thankful, we can start with a verse from the Book of Hebrews. You may think at first

I'm not talking about saying "Thank you" upon receiving a compliment or a birthday present. That's common courtesy or politeness. I'm talking about the gratitude that permeates a person's being, not only politely expressed but also deeply experienced.

it has nothing to do with gratitude, but take a moment to read it:

> Therefore, since we are receiving a kingdom which cannot be shaken, let us have grace, by which we may serve God acceptably with reverence and godly fear (12:28, *NKJV*).

There is a remarkable difference between this translation of the passage and that of the *New International Version*. Where the *New King James Version* reads, "Let us have grace," the NIV reads, "Let us be thankful." Each of these, however, is a correct translation—because in Greek to have grace (*charis*) is to say, "Thank you."

Grace and thankfulness are connected. In giving thanks, we receive grace. When we are unthankful, we are out of God's grace. This is important: We cannot enjoy God's grace without being thankful. Whether we say, "Let us be thankful," or "Let us have grace," we are really saying the same thing. So grace and gratitude connect.

Allow me to point out another interesting word origin. Thanksgiving comes from the same root word as "think." People who are thankful must set their minds to it. The attitude of gratitude does not come naturally. Thankfulness needs to be a conscious, deliberate striving. It is a matter of constantly "counting your blessings."

Why the Attitude of Gratitude?

Scripture abounds with encouragement to be thankful. "Let the peace of Christ rule in your hearts, since as members of one body you were called to peace. And be thankful" (Col. 3:15). "Be anxious for nothing, but in everything by prayer and supplication, with thanksgiving, let your requests be made known to God" (Phil. 4:6, NKJV). The apostle Paul advised the church at Thessalonica: "Give thanks in all circumstances; for this is the will of God in Christ Jesus for you" (1 Thess. 5:18, NRSV). Thankfulness is a prerequisite for worship: "Enter into his gates with thanksgiving, and into his courts with praise: be thankful" (Ps. 100:4, KJV).

More than Simply Because the Bible Tells Me So

The Scripture's encouragement to be thankful is enough for some people, but it's important to remember that being thankful isn't right just because the Bible says so. The Bible says to give thanks because it's the right way to live.

Think about it. Who really wants to be around someone who isn't grateful? The most unloving, repulsive person I know is an arrogant man who thinks he is in complete control. He puts down his wife by ignoring her. He can't keep a staff in business because he thinks everyone but himself is a bumbling fool. His philosophy is "If you want it done right, do it yourself." He takes all the credit for anything accomplished and none of the blame for anything gone wrong. He is totally ungrateful.

Yes, just as it's easy to be around grateful people, the opposite is also true. No one wants to be around the ungrateful.

Finding a Grateful Date

I was returning from a speaking engagement in the San Juan Islands when the pilot of our noisy two-seater airplane said, "The most important thing about landing is the attitude of the plane."

"What did you say?" I asked.

When he repeated himself, I said, "I can't believe it! I know that attitudes affect our moods and our relationships, but I never knew that an *airplane* has an attitude."

The pilot landed and went on to explain himself. "The attitude is down when the nose of the plane is down. And the attitude is up when the nose of the plane is up. If the attitude is too high, the plane will come down with a severe bounce. And if the attitude is too low, the plane may go out of control because of excessive landing speed. The trick is to get the right attitude in spite of atmospheric conditions."

The attitude of gratitude works the same way. It must be managed. There is no automatic pilot. As you cultivate your dating relationships, be sure to consider the right attitude of your dating partner. Here are a few qualities that can tip you off to the date with an attitude of gratitude.

1. The Grateful Date Is a Blessing

The attitude of gratitude is about knowing what to value. It's about attaching importance to people. To put it yet another way, it is about knowing how to be a blessing to people. In Hebrew, *blessing* means "to bow the knee." Bowing before someone is a graphic picture of valuing that person. Isaiah asked a rhetorical question: "Shall I bow down to a block of wood?" (44:19). Of course not! There's no value in worshiping an inanimate object! But before the Lord, "every knee will bow" (45:23; Rom. 14:11). Even "at the name of Jesus every knee should bow" (Phil. 2:10).

> **Gratitude blesses another person by saying, "You are important to me. I value you."**

Notice the important principle here: Gratitude blesses another person by saying, "You are important to me. I value you." This is what the psalmist is telling us in Ps. 103:1 when he says, "Bless the Lord, O my soul: and all that is within me, bless his holy name" (KJV). In the Scriptures we are often called on to bless or value the Lord; but don't miss the examples of people blessing other people (Deut. 33:1-2; Josh. 14:13; 2 Sam. 6:18). The attitude of gratitude is a conduit of blessing to other people. The grateful person blesses people he or she appreciates by letting them know they are valued. Gratitude says, "You are special."

So after doing some self-evaluation, ask yourself: Do you or the person you're interested in dating make other people (not just each other) feel special?

This is secret number six: **Cultivate a spirit of gratitude in your life.**

2. *The Grateful Date Is Not Easily Offended*

The person who has the attitude of gratitude has a way of glossing over minor offenses and injustices. Physical pain is a good analogy for mental pain. Everyone has his or her own threshold of physical pain. Some people, like professional athletes, can learn to tolerate pain, develop a high threshold of pain, and can keep playing even when every nerve in their body screams for attention. Most of us have a low threshold and flinch at the very thought of pain. A dentist's drill makes most of us rigid and tense.

Just as we all have a threshold of physical pain, we also have our private threshold of psychic pain. Some people can take large doses of mental or emotional abuse and keep going with a genuine smile. Others are devastated by perceived wrongs and incivilities that may not have even been intentional. Some people punish "offenders" for the slightest jostle or kick in the shins. Others simply don't allow themselves time to become victims.

As you build close relationships, notice how easily the person you're interested in dating has his or her feathers ruffled. The person who has a genuine attitude of gratitude is not easily offended.

3. *The Grateful Date Rarely Complains*

Some people whine. It doesn't matter how well things are

going—they whine. There is always something to complain about if you are of a mind to find it. Some whiners complain because God put thorns on roses. He made the ground too flat or too hilly, too dry or too wet.

It's all in your perspective. Nonwhiners might be heard thanking God for putting roses among thorns and valleys between the hills. Whiners choose to see the glass half empty and complain about it.

Leslie and I live in Seattle. It is a beautiful city surrounded with lush, green foliage, bright flowers, and productive fields, all hedged by snowcapped mountain ranges. Seattle is also known for its rainfall. Seattleites (almost like "satellite," but not quite) do not particularly complain. First, the rain does not need to be shoveled like snow back east. Second, it is the rain that makes the country unbelievably beautiful. And third, one day of gorgeous sunshine on snowcapped Mount Rainier and the ridges of the Cascade and Olympic mountains, and a native Seattleite will forgive the weatherman for the weeks of prolonged wind and rain.

But for some people this rainy condition is unforgivable. I have known people whose jobs transferred them to Seattle, and they just couldn't take it. They finally quit their jobs and moved away because they could not accept the wet winter weather. Some people would rather have desert and sunshine than lush valleys and snowcapped mountains with their inevitable precipitation.

Two people wrote letters from Seattle to relatives back east on the very same day. One of them wrote, "It is a beautiful day in Seattle," while the other one wrote, "It is the first day the sun has shone in a month." And they both told the truth. The whiner discounted the day of sunshine, while the grateful person rejoiced in its splendor.

Are you a whiner? What about the person with whom you're wanting to build a relationship? Think about it. If you're wondering whether a person is grateful, look for signs of whining. Grateful people can be identified by the absence of whining and the presence of appreciation.

The Secret of Appreciation

Gratitude is not an attribute we often talk about. In fact, not much is written about this valuable quality in personality. Gratitude may be one of the best-kept secrets of a happy dating relationship. If you seek a dating partner who is working at developing an attitude of gratitude, a partner who does not just say "thank you" because it is socially acceptable, you will be well on your way to building a healthy dating relationship.

So this is my sixth challenge to you: Decide to make thanksgiving a way of life. And as you build close relationships, look for the attitude of gratitude in others.

SELF-TEST

1. **Do you make other people (not just your date) feel valued and special? Are you a blessing to others?**
   Very rarely   *All the time*
   1   2   3   4   5   6   7

2. **Do you pass over remarks that could be taken as offensive? Are you able to overlook potential insults by not reading between the lines?**
   Very rarely   *All the time*
   1   2   3   4   5   6   7

3. **Do you look on the positive side instead of complaining or whining about your circumstances?**
Very rarely   *All the time*

1	2	3	4	5	6	7

4. **Would you say you have an attitude of gratitude?**
Very rarely   *All the time*

1	2	3	4	5	6	7

Scoring

Tally the four items. There is a possible range of scores from 4 to 28. The higher the score, the more you see your date as possessing the virtue of gratitude. As always, remember that this questionnaire is only a tool to get you thinking.

Something to Think and Talk About

- What do you enjoy about Thanksgiving? Does your family have a tradition of expressing thanks on this day? If so, what is it?

- There is a French proverb that says, "Gratitude is the heart's memory." What do you think that might mean?

- Do you ever feel thankful for something and then not say anything about it? Can you remember some examples? Why do you think it is sometimes difficult to express our appreciation and gratitude?

- Do you agree that gratitude starts in our heads? What about consistent thankfulness or what we have been calling the attitude of gratitude? Why does it have to start with thinking?

- This chapter has discussed three qualities of gratitude: being a blessing, not being easily offended, and being positive. What other characteristics of the person who is consistently appreciative can you think of?

For Further Study

Jeremy Taylor said, "From David learn to give thanks for everything. Every furrow in the Book of Psalms is sown with the seeds of thanksgiving." Set some time aside to see if Mr. Taylor is right. Select a few psalms at random, and make a list of what they have to say about the attitude of gratitude.

·8·

No, Please—You First

Submit to one another out of reverence for Christ.—EPH. 5:21

ODDSMAKERS say chances are 5 in 10 that a marriage will end in divorce. If one or both partners are still teenagers, they say the odds for divorce are even higher. If either partner witnessed an unhappy marriage at home, the odds increase again. If one or both partners come from broken homes, the odds rise yet higher. If either partner has been divorced, the odds soar. If there has been regular sexual involvement before marriage, or if either or both partners use alcohol or drugs, the odds skyrocket.

Keith and Ashley knew the odds were stacked in their favor—relatively speaking. They were sophomores in college and had been dating for nearly two years. Both came from healthy homes where mom and dad were happily married. Keith and Ashley had never used alcohol or drugs. They struggled with sexual temptation but had remained faithful to their commitment of sexual abstinence. The odds, as I said, were stacked in their favor. They were beginning to think about marriage. That's when they came to me for counsel.

Early in their first interview both of them began to recite the statistical odds I have just mentioned. Both had taken a marriage and family class, studied the sociology of marriage, and, based on the textbook, they felt they had found the love of their life.

But there was one unresolved issue—an important one—that gave me concern about their chances for making their love last a lifetime. Ashley was majoring in journalism and had dreams of working for a local newspaper as a reporter. Both her mom and dad were in the newspaper business, and she was eager to follow in her mother's footsteps. Ashley was passionate about her future career and was serious about building a professional résumé. But I noticed that whenever Ashley discussed having a career, Keith, to put it mildly, never took her seriously. He would yawn or roll his eyes or just plain ignore her.

"You don't seem very interested in Ashley's career," I observed.

"It's not that," Keith said. He went on to tell me that he always saw himself as the breadwinner in his future home, and the thought of his wife having a career was something that did not fit his picture of marriage. As the three of us talked in my office, Keith eventually blurted out something that caught both of them by surprise: "I would never allow my wife to go to work!"

"What?" Ashley's eyes became as big as saucers. "You would never *allow* your wife to go to work? Let me get this straight: if we got married, you would decide what I could and could not do?"

Well, as you might guess, Keith and Ashley never did get engaged. Eventually, each realized he or she had a different understanding of the inner workings of marriage and was not willing to compromise. That's a good lesson to learn before it's too late.

Keith and Ashley were fortunate. Many dating partners thinking about marriage never talk about their values, particularly the ones on which they won't compromise. It is easy but wrong to assume both partners have the same picture of what their relationship would be like it if were to progress.

What your dating partner values is extremely important. I often have couples write down their values and then prioritize them. I ask them to draw a line between the nonnegotiable values and the ones they are willing to adjust. This exercise helps couples discover the seventh secret to building close relationships. Once again, it's found in Ephesians: **"Submit to one another out of reverence for Christ"** (Eph. 5:21).

If a dating relationship is to lead to a healthy courtship, it will be because both people understand the principle of mutual submission. It will be because both know how to empty themselves of their self-centered desires to help the other person get his or her needs met.

What Is Mutual Submission?

There is a story of a man who dreamed he died and found himself immediately in a large room. In the room, a huge banquet table was filled with all sorts of delicious food. Around the banquet table sat obviously hungry people. The chairs, however, were five feet from the edge of the table, and the people apparently could not get out of the chairs to get to the food.

There was one single large spoon, five feet long. Everyone was fighting, quarreling, pushing each other, trying to grab that spoon. Finally, in an awful scene, one strong bully took control of the spoon. He reached out, picked up some food, and turned it to feed himself, only to find that the spoon was so long he could not touch his mouth. The food fell off. Immediately, someone else grabbed the spoon and held it. The new owner reached to pick up the food, but again could not feed himself. The handle was too long.

The man who was observing it all said to his guide, "This is hell—to have food and not be able to eat it."

The guide replied, "Where do you think you are? This *is* hell. But this is not your place. Come with me."

And they went into another room. In this room he saw a long table also filled with food, exactly as in the other room. Everyone was seated in chairs, and for some reason they too were unable to reach the food on the table.

But there was a big difference. These people had a satisfied, pleasant look on their faces. Only then did the visitor see the reason why. Exactly as before, there was only one spoon. It too had a handle five feet long. Yet no one was fighting for it. In fact, one man, who held the handle, reached out, picked up the food, and put it into the mouth of someone else, who ate it and was satisfied.

That person then took the spoon by the handle, reached for the food from the table, and put it to the mouth of the man who had just given him something to eat. And the guide said, "This is heaven."

Mutual submission is the act of emptying ourselves of self-centered desires to help other persons meet their needs. Mutual submission is not giving up our core values. It is putting ourselves aside to make room for others' needs. Mutually submissive people help each other. They are like the rails of a train track. Each is autonomous, but one is useless without the other. Without submission, a growing relationship can be tripped up by selfishness.

Why Mutual Submission?

Tim, a young man who was recently married, invited me to lunch one day and asked, "How can I get my wife to submit to me?" His question threw me. I have counseled many newlyweds on this topic but had never heard the question phrased so bluntly.

Tim was a devout Christian trying to build his new marriage on biblical principles, and he wanted to be the head of the home. He read about headship in the verse that reads, "The husband is the head of the wife as Christ is the head of the church, his body" (Eph. 5:23). Tim interpreted this statement to mean it was his job to be the boss of his wife. And in that same vein, he felt it was her job to be submissive to his demands. Tim's wife, as you might imagine, didn't see things that way. She saw herself as an equal partner in the marriage.

Tim, as sincere as he was, didn't fully understand what it meant to be "the head of the wife as Christ is the head of the church." It never seemed to occur to him that in the Bible the husband is never called to *make* his wife submit. The Bible calls husbands to rule over their homes, not their wives. It's the difference between administrating and dictating.

Submission is the job of both husband and wife. It calls men to renounce the desire to be master and be the first to honor and respect their wives. Wives should reciprocate accordingly. And all of this submission is out of respect and reverence for Christ.

What is headship, then? Let me tell you what I told Tim. Headship is not being the first in line. It is not being the boss or ruler. It is being the first to honor, the first to nurture, the first to meet the other's needs. A true administrator is also a servant.

> **Without submission every relationship, no matter how romantic, will eventually falter—even if it continues as a relationship.**

A healthy relationship, whether in dating or marriage, is built on a mutual desire to submit one's needs to the other. Emptying ourselves of our self-centered desires is the bridge to a deeper and more meaningful relationship. Without submission every relationship, no matter how romantic, will eventually falter—even if it continues as a relationship. As Amos 3:3 says, "Do two walk together unless they have agreed to do so?"

Finding a Mutually Submissive Date

If a person is to contribute to a healthy dating relationship, it will be because of understanding mutual submission. To help identify this quality in people, look for the following important characteristics—clues to whether a person understands and can practice mutual submission.

1. The Mutually Submissive Date Is Gentle

Remember the Aesop's fable in which the wind and the sun argued over which was the strongest? The wind said, "Do you see that old man down there? I can make him take his coat off quicker than you can."

The sun agreed to go behind a cloud while the wind blew up a storm. However, the harder the wind blew, the firmer the old man wrapped his coat around him.

Eventually, the wind gave up, and the sun came out from behind the cloud and smiled kindly upon the old man. Before long, the old man mopped his brow, pulled off his coat, and strolled along his way. The sun knew the secret: warmth, friendliness, and a gentle touch are always stronger than force and fury.

Some people make demands of others. Like a blowing wind, they force themselves and their needs on others. Consequently, their gains are always at the expense of others. They don't care how other people feel as long as they can immediately get their own way.

But that's not the case with the people who understand mutual submission. They make their needs known gently. They do not bulldoze their needs into the relationship. They warmly and appropriately make their requests known and balance them against the needs of their partner.

2. The Mutually Submissive Date Is Other-Oriented

It is wonderful to be with someone who feels good about who he or she is, who can throw back his or her head, breathe deeply, and enjoy life. The healthy person is not unduly concerned over the impression he or she makes on others.

No one intentionally wants to look bad in the eyes of others. What I'm saying here is that someone obsessed with the impression he or she makes on others can quickly become obnoxious. He or she is silently repeating a consuming question: "How am I doing?" That person's need for validation can pull the life out of everyone with whom he or she comes in contact.

The person not unduly concerned with the impression he or she makes on others is in the business of making other people feel at ease. He or she is more likely to ask, "How are you doing?" Such a person is more interested in making others feel at ease than in impressing people.

3. The Mutually Submissive Date Is Not Overly Competitive

Every relationship, including dating, is fueled by the twin engines of cooperation and competition. People cooperate with others for the sake of a smooth relationship. But even while we cooperate, competitive juices never completely shut off. And all it takes for competition to spill over into cooperation is a perceived threat to our self-worth. Then competition runs rampant.

> **Every relationship, including dating, is fueled by the twin engines of cooperation and competition.**

A competitive spirit can be an advantage in sports or even in careers, but when relationships are fueled primarily by competition, turbulence is certain. Competition is deadweight in any dating relationship. If, for example, another couple's expensive tastes ignite the competitive spirit of your dating partner, attention may focus on matching or outdoing that couple instead of focusing on simply developing the relationship as it stands. A healthy individual does not feel a deep need to keep up with the Joneses.

Success and failure are the children born of competition. Where one exists, so does the other. Genuinely submissive individuals enjoy the successes of others. It is a real mark of maturity on the part of any individual when he or she can genuinely appreciate the achievements of those with whom he or she makes comparisons.

It takes a lot more grace to enjoy the successes of our friends than it does to comfort them in times of disaster. And it's also easy to explain away their higher status and greater success as good luck or personal scheming. But a cooperative person sets aside competitive urges, forgoes making excuses, and enjoys others' good fortune.

Borrowing Moccasins. I know of a woman who took her five-year-old son shopping in a large department store during the Christmas season. She knew it would be fun for him to see all the decorations, window displays, toys, and Santa Claus. As she dragged him by the hand, twice as fast as his little legs could move, he began to fuss and cry. "What's the matter with you?" she scolded impatiently. "I brought you with me to have fun. Santa doesn't bring toys to little crybabies!"

His fussing continued as she rushed to find bargains. "I'm not going to take you shopping with me ever again if you don't stop whimpering," she admonished. "Oh, well—maybe it's because your shoes are untied and you're tripping over your own laces." As she knelt down beside him in the aisle to tie his shoes, she happened to look up. For the first time, she viewed a large department store through the eyes of her five-year-old. From that position she couldn't see the decorations and the toys on display. All she could see was a maze of counters too high to be visible by a small child.

Rather than fun, the scene was absolutely terrifying! It looked like a lot of rushing and crushing, shoving and bumping. Once she saw the world from the little boy's perspective, she took him home and vowed never again to impose her version of a good time on him.

When the mother experienced the department store as her little son did, she also experienced empathy—the ability to put oneself in another person's position and see the world from his or her perspective. Empathy, by the way, is sometimes confused with sympathy, but it's very different. Sympathy is standing on the shore and throwing a life ring to a person who is drowning. Empathy is diving into the water to help the person who is struggling. Sympathy is feeling sorry for someone. Empathy is putting oneself in the person's situation to understand his or her feelings.

The Sioux have a prayer about empathy. It reads: "O Great Spirit, grant me the wisdom to walk in another's moccasins before I criticize or pass judgment on what they do." The person who understands mutual submission knows how to walk in another person's shoes.

Submitting to Counsel

In their book *Fit to Be Tied,* Bill and Lynne Hybels warn against the risk of dating anyone who is a rugged individualist, not prone to submission. They write that some couples are quick to say, "'We know we're right for each other. We don't need or want your approval. So stop butting into our lives!' With that attitude, they systematically cut themselves off from the input of those who may be the most caring and insightful people in their world—their parents and trusted friends."

The Hybels go on to say that the Bible challenges rugged individualists with words like these: "Submitting yourselves one to another" (Eph. 5:21, KJV) and "In the multitude of counselors there is safety" (Prov. 11:14, NKJV).

As you think about this concept of submission with a person you're currently dating or are interested in dating, consider the value of submitting to outside counsel. An outside viewpoint can be refreshing and eye-opening. With counsel, your chances for finding true love are greatly improved. Without the quality of submission, your relationship will inevitably end in a series of power struggles.

So this is my seventh challenge to you: Empty yourself of the need to change others. Promise yourself as you build close relationships that you will discover and practice together with someone the joy of mutual submission.

SELF-TEST

1. I'm more like a dune buggy than a bulldozer. T F
2. I'm generally tender and gentle. T F
3. I try to understand people before judging them. T F
4. I usually ask how others are doing. T F
5. I genuinely enjoy the successes of others. T F
6. I'm more cooperative than competitive. T F
7. I practice the fine art of empathy. T F
8. I've learned how to avoid being self-centered. T F
9. I'm open to negotiation and compromise. T F
10. I'm generally very sensitive to the needs of others. T F

Total of T (true) responses _____

Scoring

Tally the number of "true" responses. There are 10 possible. The more you believe are true, the more you see yourself as a person who understands and practices mutual submission. Remember: this questionnaire is only a tool to get you thinking.

Something to Think and Talk About

- Even if a couple have everything going for them, how could the principle of mutual submission work to better their relationship?
- How do you think a person can empty himself or herself of self-centered desires? How can emptying oneself improve a dating relationship?
- What do you think about headship in marriage? How would you define this concept in specific terms?
- How would you explain the difference between empathy and sympathy? Which would you rather be on the receiving end of, and why?
- This chapter pointed out gentleness, empathy, other orientation, and a lack of over competitiveness as clues to a mutually submissive spirit. What other qualities do you feel are important?

For Further Study

Make a study of what Scripture has to say about the practice of self-sacrifice and self-denial. Here are a few places to study: Matt. 16:24-25; Rom. 15:1; 1 Cor. 10:24; Gal. 5:24; Phil. 2:4. You may also want to study biblical examples of unselfishness. Here are some: Abraham (Gen. 13:9); Joseph (Gen. 50:21); Jonathan (1 Sam. 18:4); Paul (1 Cor. 10:33); Christ (2 Cor. 8:9).

Conclusion

Finding True Love

Be very careful, then, how you live—not as unwise but as wise, making the most of every opportunity, because the days are evil. Therefore do not be foolish, but understand what the Lord's will is. Do not get drunk on wine, which leads to debauchery. Instead, be filled with the Spirit. Speak to one another with psalms, hymns and spiritual songs. Sing and make music in your heart to the Lord, always giving thanks to God the Father for everything, in the name of our Lord Jesus Christ. Submit to one another out of reverence for Christ.

—EPH. 5:15-21

So this is my final challenge to you: Focus not on seeking out the perfect dating partner, but on becoming the perfect dating partner. Promise yourself that you will strive to embody the seven secrets: wisdom, optimism, discernment, spirituality, joyfulness, gratitude, and empathy.

Here are some final thoughts as you contemplate building relationships.

You will never find (or be) the perfect date. No person will ever exactly match the biblical ideals discussed in this book. No human being consistently embodies all seven qualities—wisdom, optimism, discernment, spirituality, joyfulness, gratitude, and empathy.

There are people who are much closer to achieving these qualities than others, but no one is perfect. So don't waste time searching for the perfect date. He or she doesn't exist. We're all still growing, still learning, still becoming who God intends us to be.

If you spend all your time searching for Mr. or Ms. Perfect, you'll be headed in the wrong direction. Cut yourself and your potential date some slack. Take plenty of time and space to grow.

Changing Directions

Russian novelist Leo Tolstoy said, "Everybody thinks of changing humanity, but nobody thinks of changing himself." He could have said the same thing about dating.

To find a great date, don't try to make someone into an

ideal partner. Instead, put your energy into being a better person yourself. Cultivate the seven qualities of a great date in your own life. Here's a quick review.

Secret 1: WISDOM

Descartes wrote, "Common sense is the best distributed commodity in the world, for every man is convinced that he is well supplied with it." That may be true, but the common sense of wisdom is too often lacking among dating relationships.

Wendy, 18, wrote from Texas to tell me about her boyfriend. She loved him deeply. But he treated her like dirt. He was insanely jealous, obsessively possessive, verbally abusive, and painfully destructive. Wendy went on to explain that she had not been happy for the past six months, but she still loved him. What should she do? The answer may be obvious to you and me, but not to Wendy. She needed to end the relationship, but she lacked the wisdom to see things clearly.

That's a critical part of wisdom—being able to be objective with yourself. It's tough to do, and all of us need help in seeing our own situation as it really is. But there is good news: "If any of you lacks wisdom, he should ask God, who gives generously to all without finding fault, and it will be given to him" (James 1:5).

So make a list of things you need more wisdom on. Ask God to direct you in your decision making. By the way, God often makes His wisdom known through other people's counsel. Are there people—a teacher, a youth pastor, or a friend, for example—who might help you cultivate wisdom? Put their names next to the things on your list, and devise an action plan for achieving wisdom.

Secret 2: OPTIMISM

Karl Menninger said, "Attitudes are more important than facts." Why? Because you can't change the facts, but you *can* change your attitude—that's the point of optimism. It's an attitude that allows us to adjust to things beyond our control. Many things in life are beyond our control—eye color, race, earthquakes in southern California—but our attitude is not one of them. We can choose to be optimistic.

There is a short poem that reminds me of the importance of keeping a positive outlook while being adjustable. It was written by Gail Brook Burket and is one of my favorites:

> I do not ask to walk smooth paths
> Nor bear an easy load,
> I pray for strength and fortitude
> To climb the rock-strewn road.
>
> Give me such courage I can scale
> The hardest peaks alone,
> And transform every stumbling block
> Into a stepping-stone.

One of the basic ideas we learn from the Bible is that life is not always fair or logical. We live in a spiritual world that defies hard facts and logical conclusions. In this life there are evil days. That's when we need hope, an optimism from God. So I ask you: What are you doing to cultivate optimism in your life? Make a list of specific areas where you are perhaps more cynical or pessimistic than need be. Think through what optimism would look like for each of those areas.

Secret 3: DISCERNMENT

In the mid-1960s, FBI Director J. Edgar Hoover was reading a typed copy of a letter he had just dictated to his secretary. He didn't like the way she had formatted the letter, so he scribbled on the bottom, "Watch the borders," and asked her to retype it and send it to his top agents. That afternoon the secretary did as she was instructed and sent the letter out. For the next two weeks FBI agents were put on special alert along the Canadian and Mexican borders.

Have you ever misunderstood someone's directions? Have you ever made a foolish mistake? We all have. It's human to make mistakes. But when it comes to being in God's will, there is no place for error. Consider again what Paul said: "Do not be foolish, but understand what the Lord's will is" (Eph. 5:17).

In chapter 4 we defined the Lord's will as imitating God's love (Eph. 5:1-2). So I want to ask you: What are you doing to imitate God's love? Since that requires some reflection, take a few moments to respond. Fold a sheet of paper in two. On one half, write down what you have recently done to imitate God's love. On the other half, write down some of the ways you could imitate His love in the future.

Of course, to discern God's will and imitate Him in specific situations, you will need to study His Word, pray, and worship. And you will want to ask yourself, "What would Jesus do if He were in my place?"

Earlier I suggested that you ask, "When I am around the person I am dating, am I more like Jesus?" But now I want to encourage you also to ask, "When the person I am dating is around me, is he or she more like Jesus because of me and my behavior?"

Secret 4: SPIRITUALITY

In chapter 5 we talked about the fullness of the Spirit. We talked about a date having an "internal orientation" and not being dependent on externals for happiness. Allow me to turn the tables. Are you looking only on the surface of things? Are you looking only at externals to find happiness, or do you rely on Christ to supply your needs? Let me ask it straight out: What are you doing to be filled with the Holy Spirit?

I offer a distinction that helped me become more Spirit-filled. I used to think that if I was going to be really spiritual, I should work at removing everything from my life that was not spiritual. So I tried to keep all the rules and do everything just right. But the pressure wore me out. I was on the verge of giving up when I read about a sermon preached by Dwight L. Moody. He used an illustration that showed me how the Holy Spirit works.

Moody held up a glass jar to his congregation and asked, "How can I get the air out of this jar?" People didn't know what to say. Finally one man shouted, "You could seal the top and use a pump to suck it out." Moody replied, "That would create a vacuum and shatter the glass." The crowd was once again silent. Finally Moody smiled, picked up a pitcher of water, and filled the glass jar. "There," he said. "All the air is now removed." He then went on to show that the way to an effective Christian life is not by trying to be perfect, but rather by being filled with the Spirit.

Do you sometimes feel defeated because you're working on overcoming by yourself rather than relying on the infilling of the Holy Spirit? Ask God to fill you continually with His Spirit. This is His will. "This is the will of God, even your sanctification" (1 Thess. 4:3, KJV).

Secret 5: JOYFULNESS

Blessed is he who has learned to laugh at himself, for he shall never cease to be entertained. You don't need to have comic timing or know how to tell a good joke to have joy. You don't even need to smile, although it helps.

A 12-year-old Canadian girl in Winnipeg holds the record for smiling. She smiled for 10 hours and 5 minutes straight, beating the longest smile recorded in the *Guinness Book of World Records* of 7 hours, 32 minutes. I don't know if that girl is joyful or not, for joy is much deeper than a smile. As beautiful as a smile is, it's not the test of joy. Joy does not depend on circumstances. It is an attitude that defies difficult situations—even on "evil days."

In chapter 6 I reported on an important sentence I read in a textbook on marriage. It said, *"The most important character-*

istic of a marriageable person is the habit of happiness." When happiness becomes a habit, joy is born. What are you doing to make happiness a habit? Are you learning to be positive, content, and adjustable? Or are you waiting passively for something or someone to make you happy? Consider these three qualities of joy (you may want to review the last part of chapter 6), and jot down a few thoughts about how you practice them in your daily life. If you work on these three traits of joy for two weeks, you will soon make them a habit.

Secret 6: GRATEFULNESS

I have a friend who owns a business with more than 100 employees. At Thanksgiving he sent each of his employees a choice turkey. He told me that out of all his employees, only four thanked him, two by written notes, and two said "Thanks" when they chanced to meet him in the hall. This business owner then told me, "If you want to find gratitude, look for it in the dictionary."

Gratitude is sometimes hard to come by, especially with any kind of consistency. In chapter 7 I told you to seek out a dating partner who has an attitude of gratitude—not someone who is simply courteous, but someone who has made gratitude a way of life, someone who is grateful for each day of life and all the little, unexpected blessings it brings.

Once again I reverse the direction and ask if *you* have an attitude of gratitude. Do you take time to appreciate the simple things in life? Do you appreciate sunshine, friendship, good books, laughter, warm fires—the so-called ordinary things of life? Gratitude makes life richer. I have observed patients in a hospital recover from near-death accidents and become grateful for every morsel of life. It doesn't take a tragedy, however, to cultivate the attitude of gratitude.

So I ask you: What are you doing to be more grateful? As you consider your answer, focus on the blessings you receive from God and from others. Make a list of things you are grateful for. Make a list of things you thank God for, and a list of things you thank people in your life for. This may help you savor each blessing and build an attitude of gratitude.

Secret 7: **EMPATHY**

In chapter 8 we talked about emptying ourselves of selfish desires. We talked about empathy as an essential part of love. Without empathy we can never accurately understand another person. Paul Tournier said, "He who loves understands, and he who understands loves." Without empathy, all our attempts to meet another's needs are flawed.

Everyone is born with the capacity to empathize. Even children as young as two will turn a picture so others can see it or bring a favorite toy to an upset friend. But we don't always tap into our capacity for empathy, because it takes effort. Empathy combines our abilities to analyze as well as sympathize. It involves a delicate balance between the head and the heart. Empathy is putting yourself in the shoes of another person and looking out at the world through that person's glasses. Empathy seeks understanding of the home he or she grew up in, the unique pressure he or she copes with, the fears he or she holds tightly, and so on.

Empathy is always risky because it will change you. And change is frightening. I have seen medical doctors scoff at the annoyance of patients who are concerned about their medical treatment. I have also seen some of those same doctors in the patient role. When they become ill and are concerned about their own health, they become irritated at the slightest hint of not being properly cared for. Once they have entered the world of the patient, they learn empathy and emerge as different doctors.

Try empathy for yourself. Take a moment to empathize with the person who brings you the most grief. Use both your head and your heart. If you exert the effort to understand another's world as that person does, with all its problems, your attitude will change. You will be far less likely to pass judgment.

How can you make empathy a permanent part of your character? Take a moment to list three or four people with whom you would like to empathize better.

The Spin Cycle

"How much is this bottle of Tide?" the young boy asked the clerk.

"What are you going to do with that big bottle?" he responded.

"Wash my cat!"

"Wash your cat? You shouldn't wash your cat with that soap. It's much too strong."

> **An additional secret to building a close relationship with someone is this: Become the kind of person you're looking for!**

But the boy insisted on his purchase. When he returned to the store a few days later, the clerk inquired about the cat.

"Oh, he died," said the boy.

"Sorry to hear that. But I warned you not to use Tide."

"Aw, the soap didn't hurt him a bit," the boy replied. "It was the spin cycle that got him!"

Dating has its own spin cycle. The excitement, anticipation, expectations, dashed hopes, demands, and pressure can be turned on too high and swirl around and around at dizzying speeds. And many individuals accelerate the problem by jumping into the spin cycle without knowing its direction. They get involved in a relationship, never knowing what they want or even who they are.

By anchoring yourself with the seven qualities of wisdom, optimism, discernment, spirituality, joyfulness, gratitude, and empathy, you are sure to avoid some of the dizzying motion of dating. And you are far more likely to find true love.

An additional secret to building a close relationship with someone is this: **Become the kind of person you're looking for!** Did you catch that? As you develop these qualities, you increase your likelihood of finding someone who wants to spend time with you.

The point of Paul's message in Ephesians 5 is to make you a better person. Read it again with your name in the spaces of my paraphrase.

- Be careful, then, how you live, _____, not as unwise, but as wise.
- Make the most of every opportunity, _____, because these are evil days.
- And don't be foolish either, _____, but understand what the Lord's will is.
- Do not get drunk with wine, which leads to debauchery; _____, but be filled with the Spirit.
- Speak to one another with psalms, hymns, and spiritual songs. Sing and make music in your heart to the Lord, _____.
- _____, always give thanks to God the Father for everything in the name of our Lord Jesus Christ.
- And finally, _____, submit to others out of reverence for Christ.

Don't ever stop looking for these qualities in others. Encourage them in your friends, your family members, and especially in yourself. Develop them in yourself and make them a part of your own character.

Something to Think and Talk About

- Do you agree with the idea that to *find* a great date you have to *become* a great date? Why or why not?
- Out of the seven qualities of a great date—wisdom, optimism, discernment, spirituality, joyfulness, gratitude, and empathy—which one or two is most important to you? Why?

- Out of the seven qualities of a great date, which one or two are most often neglected as a topic of discussion? Why?
- Out of the seven qualities of a great date, which one or two do you feel you need to work on most?
- How does focusing on *being* a great date (instead of *seeking* a great date) prevent one from falling into the "spin cycle" of feeling out of control?

For Further Study

- Take time to review each of the seven qualities discussed in earlier chapters. What specific characteristics combine to make up each of these qualities? As you study each one, use a separate sheet of paper to devise a specific plan for how you can improve that quality within yourself.